MICROPROCESSOR OPERATING SYSTEMS

VOLUME III

MICROPROCESSOR OPERATING SYSTEMS

VOLUME III

Edited by John Zarrella

MICROCOMPUTER APPLICATIONS

Suisun City, California

MICROCOMPUTER APPLICATIONS
P.O. Box E, Suisun City, California 94585

Copyright © 1984 by MICROCOMPUTER APPLICATIONS

Note:

Access Manager, ASM-86, Concurrent CP/M, CP-NET, DDT-86, Digital Research C,
    Display Manager, Digital Research FORTRAN-77, LIB-86, LINK-86, Pascal/MT+,
    Personal BASIC, RASM-86, SID-86, and XREF-86 are trademarks of Digital Research Inc.
CP/M, CP/M-86, and CBASIC are registered trademarks of Digital Research Inc.
MS-DOS is a trademark of Microsoft, Inc.
MSP, OS/ENGINE, and MSP/68000 are trademarks of Hemenway Corporation.
PICK and ACCESS are trademarks of PICK SYSTEMS.
FORTH and polyFORTH are registered trademarks of FORTH, Inc.
p-System, Universal Operating System, and Universal Medium are trademarks of SofTech
    Microsystems, Inc.
RM/COS is a registered trademark of Ryan-McFarland Corporation.
SuperDOS and CODECHEK are trademarks of Bluebird Systems.
TurboDOS is a trademark of Software 2000.
iRMX, iSBC, iSBX and the combination of iRMX, iSBC, iSBX, or MCS with a
    numerical suffix are trademarks of Intel Corporation.
Intellec, MCS, and Multibus are registered trademarks of Intel Corporation.
Idris is a trademark of Whitesmiths, Ltd.
I/OS is a trademark of InfoSoft Systems, Inc.
OASIS and OASIS-16 are trademarks of Phase One Systems, Inc.
VRTX is a trademark of Hunter & Ready, Inc.
VERSAdos is a trademark of Motorola, Inc.
UNIX is a trademark of Bell Laboratories.
Ada is a trademark of the U.S. Department of Defense (Ada Joint Program Office).
Z80 is a trademark of Zilog, Inc.
DEC and PDP are trademarks of Digital Equipment Corporation.
IBM is a registered trademark of International Business Machines Corporation.
CIS COBOL and LEVEL II COBOL are trademarks of Micro Focus, Inc.
UCSD Pascal is a registered trademark of the Regents of the University of California.

Library of Congress Cataloging in Publication Data
(Revised for Volume III)
Main entry under title:

Microprocessor operating systems.

    Includes bibliographical references and index.
    1. Operating systems (Computers) 2. Microprocessors.
I. Zarrella, John.
QA76.6.M486   001.64'25   81-80864
ISBN 0-935230-03-3 (pbk. : v. 1)

ISBN 0-935230-10-6

Printed in the United States of America
10 9 8 7 6 5 4 3 2 1

CONTENTS

PREFACE

The availability of well-designed and proven system software is a fundamental requirement for the effective utilization of today's advanced microprocessor systems. By far the most important (and visible) system software package is the operating system—a collection of software modules that manages system resources, permits user tasks to interface to system hardware, and provides services that allow tasks to interact in a straightforward, efficient, and reliable manner. This book is the third volume in a series describing the most important microprocessor operating systems currently available.

The Microprocessor Operating System Series is designed for system engineers and managers who must evaluate, select, and/or design operating systems to support applications software. A complete chapter is dedicated to each operating system. In this volume, the Concurrent CP/M, MS-DOS, MSP, PICK, PolyFORTH, p-System, RM/COS, SuperDOS, and TurboDOS operating systems are described. Most chapters are written by an industry leader involved in the development or implementation of the operating system, ensuring an accurate and complete exposition. Similar chapter formats permit the systems to be easily compared and contrasted. In addition, each chapter presents a concise functional overview of the appropriate system as well as many user-oriented technical details.

Chapter I provides a brief introduction to the history of the systems in this volume. Chapters 2 through 10 contain descriptions of existing microprocessor operating systems. Most chapters also contain a number of specific references for follow-up research on the system described in the text.

This book is intended to be used as a companion volume to **Operating Systems: Concepts and Principles.** Readers unfamiliar with general operating system concepts may wish to refer to **Operating Systems: Concepts and Principles** for terminology definitions and for an overview of operating system fundamentals.

I am extremely indebted to a number of individuals who helped to make this book a reality, especially Mike Busch, Shel Fung, Eileen Cagney Hemenway, and Kay Sakata. I would also like to thank the authors of the operating system chapters for their excellent contributions.

                                                                    J.Z.

Chapter 1

INTRODUCTION

Concurrent
CP/M

MS-DOS

MSP

PICK

polyFORTH

p-System

RM/COS

SuperDOS

TurboDOS

1

This volume describes nine popular operating systems for microprocessor systems—the Concurrent CP/M, MS-DOS, MSP, PICK, polyFORTH, p-System, RM/COS, SuperDOS, and TurboDOS operating systems. The nine operating system chapters can be read in any order. Also, to aid in obtaining additional information about the systems described in this book, most of the chapters contain a list of references. These references can be used as a starting point for further research.

The remainder of this chapter provides a brief history of each system.

The Concurrent CP/M Operating System

The history of Digital Research's operating system products dates back to 1975 when Gary Kildall implemented an early version of CP/M as a run-time support system for Intel's PL/M-80 high-level language. This CP/M version was one of the first operating systems developed for microcomputer systems. Today, the CP/M operating system has been implemented on hundreds of different systems using 8080, 8085, and Z80 processors.

The original CP/M operating system was followed by a multitasking system and a networking system. More recently, in 1980, Digital Research introduced CP/M-86—a single user/single task operating system. Designed for the Intel 8086/8088 processor family, CP/M-86 is available for many 16-bit computers, including the IBM PC.

Finally, Concurrent CP/M was introduced by Digital Research in October of 1982. Concurrent CP/M expands on CP/M-86 capabilities by allowing a single user to execute multiple tasks. In May of 1983, the generic (OEM) version of Concurrent CP/M was released and in July, Concurrent CP/M was updated to support the IBM PC XT.

The MS-DOS Operating System

The MS-DOS operating system was originally developed by Seattle Computer Products (under the name 86-DOS) for use with its 8086 computer systems. This operating system was designed so that existing CP/M-80 programs could be translated into 8086 programs (via Intel's translation rules) and execute under 86-DOS without other modifications.

In 1981, Microsoft purchased the rights to 86-DOS from Seattle Computer Products and renamed the system MS-DOS. IBM adopted the MS-DOS system for use on the IBM PC. Many other computer manufacturers, in order to promote IBM compatibility, have adopted the MS-DOS operating system for use on their hardware.

The MSP Operating System

The MSP operating system began with the production of Hemenway's multitasking nucleus in 1979. Using the company's software expertise, the nucleus was extended into a full-featured operating system—MSP.

The MSP operating system was initially released in January, 1981. Since that time, Hemenway Corporation has continued to upgrade the system by adding programming language compilers and interpreters.

The PICK Operating System

The PICK operating system was originally developed by Dick Pick (while he was working at TRW in 1967) as part of the U.S. Army GIRLS project (Generalized Information Retrieval Language System). Pick left TRW in 1969 and continued to develop/improve his original design.

In 1972, the first commercial implementation of the PICK operating system was completed on a Microdata minicomputer. This implementation was known as the REALITY system. The first PICK implementation on a microprocessor occurred in 1982 on the DEC LSI-11.

The polyFORTH Operating System

polyFORTH is the latest in a series of FORTH-based operating systems offered by FORTH, Inc. polyFORTH was first marketed in 1979. A substantial upgrade was made in 1982. The system is available in several levels—from a relatively inexpensive hobbyist version to a complete professional system (with source code).

The polyFORTH operating system is very closely coupled to the FORTH language—indeed the polyFORTH system provides the required environment in which to execute FORTH programs. Development of the FORTH language began in 1970 at a government laboratory. In 1973, FORTH, Inc. was founded to continue development of the FORTH language and execution environment.

The p-System Operating System

Development of the p-System began as the solution to a particular problem—the University of California at San Diego needed interactive access to a high-level language for a computer science course. In late 1974, Kenneth Bowles began the development of the p-System to solve the university's problem.

The p-System project soon outgrew the university's resources. SofTech, Inc. was chosen to support and develop the p-System. In 1979, SofTech formed SofTech Microsystems to support p-System users and continue development of the system.

The RM/COS Operating System

After developing a number of COBOL compilers under contract, Ryan-McFarland designed and implemented a proprietary COBOL compiler—RM/COBOL.

Development of RM/COBOL, along with contract work on various operating system products, led to the development of the RM/COS operating system. RM/COS was designed to provide an efficient and portable business-oriented operating environment for RM/COBOL applications.

Since it was first introduced, RM/COS has been implemented on several 68000-based systems and on TI 990/9900 systems.

The SuperDOS Operating System

The SuperDOS operating system is the work of two authors—Tom Lee and David Houge. SuperDOS grew out of their consulting business. In order to provide small business users with sophisticated application software on low-cost microcomputer hardware, they developed the SuperDOS operating system.

With over ten years experience in programming business software on minicomputers, the authors designed SuperDOS for the express purpose of supporting business software. The initial versions of SuperDOS ran on Z80-based systems.

Bluebird Systems purchased exclusive rights to SuperDOS in 1982. Recently, Bluebird Systems announced SuperDOS support for the 8088-based IBM PC and XT computers.

The TurboDOS Operating System

Development of TurboDOS was begun by Software 2000 in 1980. The main goal of the design was to provide reliability and performance for a multiple user microcomputer system in a commercial environment. The designers felt that existing systems did not provide sufficient reliability and performance. TurboDOS was first introduced in April 1981. This version allowed multiple microprocessors to operate in a network configuration.

TurboDOS was originally developed for Z80-based microcomputers. It is compatible with CP/M application packages, languages, and programming tools. Recently, an expanded version of TurboDOS has been developed that supports 8086-family microprocessors. This version provides a software environment compatible with the CP/M-86 environment. The 8086 version includes an emulator for MS-DOS/PC-DOS that runs many IBM PC application programs without modification.

Chapter 2

THE CONCURRENT CP/M OPERATING SYSTEM

*A Single User, Multitasking Operating System
Designed for 8086- and 8088-based Microcomputers*

Gary Gysin
Digital Research Inc.

2

Concurrent CP/M is a single user, multitasking operating system for microcomputer systems. This operating system, developed by Digital Research, Inc., was introduced in October of 1982. Concurrent CP/M lets a single user run more than one program simultaneously. A typical business application of Concurrent CP/M enables a user to create a spreadsheet, make modifications to a memo, plot the graph created for this year's sales, and print out a previously completed document —all at the same time. Concurrent CP/M can be configured to run as many as 254 programs simultaneously.

At this time, Concurrent CP/M operates on 8086- and 8088-based microcomputers. (Future versions will be available for Motorola 68000 and Intel 80286-based machines.) Digital Research offers two Concurrent CP/M products. The first product is designed for the IBM Personal Computer and the IBM Personal Computer XT. This version is configured to run four simultaneous processes. The second version is designed for any 8086- or 8088-based system, can be configured to run up to 254 simultaneous processes, and is typically sold only to hardware manufacturers. Hardware manufacturers that have licensed Concurrent CP/M include DEC, Texas Instruments, NCR, Olivetti, Eagle, Commodore, Fujitsu, Televideo, and Vector Graphics.

Key Features

One of Concurrent CP/M's most important multitasking features is the "virtual console" concept. A virtual console can either be associated with the screen that the user is viewing or can be a portion of memory that is storing an image of another screen. The user can switch from virtual console to virtual console with the touch of a key. One virtual console, the foreground console, is always mapped to the physical console. The remaining virtual consoles (background consoles) do not have access to the physical console. By pressing a function key, the current foreground console is switched with the selected background console. Programs will continue to execute in the individual virtual consoles whether they appear on the screen or not. In a sense, Concurrent CP/M's virtual console environment executes in a manner similar to a television set. Like a television set, which lets a viewer switch between stations and view them one at a time on a single screen, Concurrent CP/M lets the user switch to and from several virtual consoles and view the currently executing programs. (See Figure 2-1.)

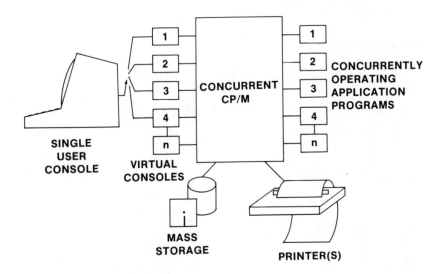

Figure 2-1   Concurrent CP/M Lets a User Connect a Single Physical Console to One of Many Virtual Consoles.

In addition to virtual consoles, Concurrent CP/M can be configured to display windows. A Concurrent CP/M window is a viewport to a virtual console. By using the Concurrent CP/M windows, the user can monitor up to 254 executing programs—on the same screen at the same time.

Background virtual consoles operate in two distinct modes: dynamic and buffered. When a background console is in dynamic mode, the operating system does not store the output of the executing program. Thus, dynamic mode operation is similar to switching stations on a television set; when a viewer switches stations, programming continues but the viewer cannot see the events that occur on any of the stations that are switched out. Buffered mode, on the other hand, lets a user store the output of a background virtual console. Concurrent CP/M will begin recording the program output when a program is switched into the background. While the program remains in the background, Concurrent CP/M records the output from the program and stores this output in a disk file. When the user switches back to the console, Concurrent CP/M displays (on the console screen) the output that was stored in the disk file. The operator sees all output generated since that task was last viewed and no information is lost.

Hardware Requirements

The hardware requirements for Concurrent CP/M include:

1) An Intel 8086 or 8088 microprocessor.

2) A console device and a real-time clock.

3) At least 256K bytes of RAM.

4) 1 to 16 disk drives of up to 512 megabytes each.

Concurrent CP/M has been designed to run on almost any configuration of 8086- or 8088-based hardware systems. The architecture of Concurrent CP/M promotes portability and consistency between different hardware systems and microprocessors.

Portability

Concurrent CP/M consists of three interface levels that are responsible for its high degree of portability: the user interface, the logically invariant software interface, and the actual hardware interface. The user interface, which Digital Research distributes, is a "resident system process" called the Terminal Message Process (TMP). (Resident system processes are programs that become part of the operating system and reside in memory at all times.) The TMP accepts command lines from the virtual consoles and executes the commands.

The logically invariant interface to the operating system (also supplied by Digital Research) consists of the system calls that handle file creation and deletion, facilitates either sequential or random file access, and allocates and frees disk space. A module of this invariant interface is called the Basic Disk Operating System (BDOS).

The third and last major component of Concurrent CP/M is the hardware interface. The eXtended Input/Output System (XIOS) communicates directly with the particular hardware environment. The XIOS is composed of a set of functions that are called by processes needing to perform physical I/O. The XIOS is usually supplied by the hardware manufacturer and consists of a set of I/O drivers that interfaces to the standard DRI-supplied operating system.

The portability of Concurrent CP/M is based upon the modularity of these three interface levels. Every computer system that runs Concurrent CP/M has the same TMP and BDOS. Software developers need not be concerned with which machine an individual Concurrent CP/M application executes on. By using standard BDOS calls, a programmer can ensure that his/her program is portable across all Concurrent CP/M-based machines. (See Figure 2-2.)

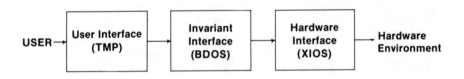

Figure 2-2   Concurrent CP/M Ensures Software Portability by Providing Three Modular Interface Levels.

The differences among Concurrent CP/M installations result from the implementation of the XIOS by the system's hardware manufacturer. The device drivers that are added to the XIOS correspond to the exact physical devices in the hardware system. (These device drivers will differ from machine to machine.)

Job/Task Control

Job and task control is handled by the Real Time Monitor (RTM). The RTM is Concurrent CP/M's real-time multitasking nucleus. The RTM performs process dispatching, queue management, flag management, device polling, and system timing tasks.

Although Concurrent CP/M is a multitasking operating system, at any given time only one process has access to the processor resource. Unless a program is specifically written to communicate or synchronize execution with other processes, a process is unaware of other processes competing for system resources. The primary task of the RTM is to transfer (or dispatch) the processor resource from one process to another. The RTM module called the Dispatcher performs this task.

Concurrent CP/M is a priority-driven system. During a dispatch, the operating system allocates the processor resource to the process with the highest priority. Concurrent CP/M supports up to 255 priority levels. The Dispatcher allots equal shares of the system's resources to processes with the same priority. With priority dispatching, the system never passes control to a lower-priority process if there is a higher-priority process on the ready list. (A ready process is one that is waiting for the processor.) Because high-priority, compute-bound processes tend to monopolize the processor, it is best to reduce their priority to avoid degrading overall system performance.

Queue management is an integral part of the RTM. A process can use a queue to communicate with another process, to synchronize its execution with that of another process, and to exclude other processes from protected system resources. A process can make, open, delete, read from, or write to a queue with system calls similar to those used to manage disk files. The queue manager in Concurrent CP/M supports communication among, and synchronization of, independently-running processes.

The Real Time Monitor also performs system timing functions. The system timing calls include keeping the time of day and delaying the execution of a process for a specified period of time. An internal process called CLOCK provides the time of day for the system. By setting a series of flags using CLOCK, a process can be delayed for any specified amount of time.

Memory Configurations

Although Concurrent CP/M is typically stored in RAM, there is nothing in the system that precludes incorporation in silicon. CP/M-86, a single user, single task operating system from Digital Research, has been stored in the 80150 chip marketed by Intel. A ROM-based operating system eliminates the traditional boot procedure of loading an operating system disk and reading its contents into RAM. The 80150 lowers overall computer production costs because a disk drive and attendant control circuits are replaced by a solitary chip. Concurrent CP/M, like CP/M-86, can be chosen for a ROM-based operating system.

Concurrent CP/M can function in a 128K-byte system, although 256K is recommended as a minimum. The operating system can support up to one megabyte of main memory and functions optimally in a hard disk-based environment.

Hardware Support

As previously stated, Concurrent CP/M supports hardware timers or real-time clocks and can delay the execution of a process for a specified period of time.

Concurrent CP/M can also be configured to execute in a multiprocessor environment. A dual processor machine can utilize the capabilities of Concurrent CP/M to run both 8-bit and 16-bit applications.

I/O Devices

Concurrent CP/M can support up to 254 character I/O devices. These I/O devices are usually printers and consoles. The flexibility of Concurrent CP/M allows any character I/O device to be added to the operating system as long as the appropriate device drivers are added to the XIOS.

Software Support

A series of high-level language compilers, programming tools, and an interpreter are available for Concurrent CP/M. The high-level language compilers that are available from Digital Research are CBASIC, Digital Research C, Pascal MT+, PL/I, CIS COBOL, LEVEL II COBOL, and Digital Research FORTRAN-77. The interpreter is Personal Basic. Digital Research also supplies many programmer tools including two subroutine library programs—Display Manager and Access Manager—that simplify the development of commercial applications. Display Manager is a tool for designing screen displays.

Access Manager is a fast, versatile, advanced file access manager. This program, used in conjunction with a native code compiler from Digital Research, enables a programmer to develop programs with B-tree index file structures.

Products that are standardly included with the purchase of Concurrent CP/M include a relocatable assembler, an assembly language cross-reference program, a linker, a software librarian that creates and manages libraries, a debugger, and a line oriented editor. These products are named RASM-86, XREF-86, LINK-86, LIB-86, DDT-86, and ED, respectively.

1) RASM-86. RASM-86 processes an 8086 assembly language source file in three passes and produces an 8086 machine language object file. RASM-86 can optionally produce three output files from one source file: LST, OBJ, and SYM. The LST list file contains the assembly language listing with any error messages. The OBJ object file contains the object code in Intel 8086 relocatable object format. The SYM symbol file lists any user-defined symbols.

2) XREF-86. XREF-86 is an assembly language cross-reference utility program that creates a cross-reference file showing the use of symbols throughout the program. XREF-86 uses the LST and SYM files created by RASM-86.

3) LINK-86. LINK-86 combines relocatable object files into a command file that runs under any of the Digital Research family of 8086-based operating systems. The object files can be produced by Digital Research's 8086 language translators, the native code compilers and relocatable assemblers, or by any other translators that produce object files using a compatible subset of the Intel 8086 object module format.

4) LIB-86. LIB-86 is a utility program for creating and maintaining library files that contain 8086 object modules. These modules can be produced by Digital Research's 8086 language translators or by any other translators that produce modules in Intel's 8086 object module format. LIB-86 can be used to create libraries, as well as append, replace, select, or delete modules

from an existing library. LIB-86 can also be used to obtain information about the contents of library files.

5) Debuggers. Digital Research supplies two debuggers, DDT-86 and SID-86. DDT-86 is the standard debugger that is supplied with Concurrent CP/M. SID-86 is a symbolic debugger that is available separately. The DDT-86 program allows a user to test and debug programs interactively in a Concurrent CP/M environment. DDT-86 lets a programmer compare blocks of memory, load a program for execution, begin execution (with optional breakpoints), search for strings, trace program execution, and examine and modify the processor state. SID-86, on the other hand, is a symbolic instruction debugger. SID-86 expands on the features of DDT-86, allowing users to test and debug programs interactively. SID-86 features include symbolic assembly and disassembly, permanent breakpoints with pass counts, and trace without call. SID-86 also accepts expressions involving hexadecimal, decimal, ASCII, and symbolic values.

6) ED. ED is a line-oriented editor. ED allows a user to create and alter Concurrent CP/M text files.

System Security

Concurrent CP/M supports password protection on directories and files. If more than one person uses a system, passwords can protect files from accidental damage by other users. Passwords also provide security for managers and systems personnel who want to limit access to particular files. Any program, command, or data file can have individual password protection. The PASSWORD option of the SET command lets the user add this protection to files.

Concurrent CP/M also supports record- and file-locking. These features are crucial in a multitasking environment where simultaneous access of the same record would cause data integrity problems. Record- and file-locking under Concurrent CP/M prevent a process from deleting, renaming, or updating the attributes of another process' open file. The lock features also prevent a process from opening a file currently opened by another process. Record- and file-locking can also prevent a process from resetting a drive on which another process has an open file.

Concurrent CP/M supports two open file modes that allow concurrently running processes to access common records. These two modes are "read-only" and "unlocked." The read only mode allows multiple processes to read from a common file; processes cannot write to a file that has been opened in this mode. Thus, files remain static when they are opened in read-only mode. The unlocked mode is more complex because it allows multiple processes to read and write records in a common file. If a file is opened in the unlocked mode, individual records or groups of records within that file may be temporarily locked by a user. A record may also be updated in the unlocked mode. In this case, before an update is performed an unaltered copy of the record in memory is compared with the record on the disk. If the disk copy has been altered, an error message is returned to the application program. Concurrent CP/M files can also be set to "locked" mode. Locked mode may be used when it is necessary to ensure that only one user may open a specific file at a given time. Once a file is opened in the locked mode, other user requests for that file are denied.

Application programs enable record- and file-locking by using BDOS calls. If an application was not written to use record- and file-locking BDOS calls, Concurrent CP/M automatically defaults to the locked mode.

Error Recovery

The Concurrent CP/M file system has extensive error handling capabilities. When an error is detected, the BDOS responds in one of three ways:

1) By returning to the calling process with return codes in the AX register that identify the error.

2) By displaying an error message on the console and terminating the process.

3) By displaying an error message on the console and returning an error code to the calling process.

The application programmer chooses the error handling method by making BDOS calls.

Logical I/O

Concurrent CP/M supports two logical devices, "CON:" and "LST:". CON: designates the physical console device. When used as a source, CON: is usually the keyboard; when used as a destination, CON: is normally the display screen. LST: designates the physical listing device—usually the printer.

System Generation

Concurrent CP/M is supplied with a sample XIOS to simplify the generation of a new system. This XIOS is configured for operation on the IBM Personal Computer with two 5¼-inch, double-density, single-sided, flexible diskette drives and at least 256K bytes of RAM. These XIOS subroutines can be modified to tailor the system to almost any 8086 or 8088 disk-based operating environment.

The steps needed to generate a Concurrent CP/M operating system are relatively straightforward:

1) Develop the XIOS assembler routines for a particular hardware configuration.

2) Edit the XIOS source file to create a customized XIOS.

3) Assemble the XIOS using the Digital Research assembler, ASM-86.

4) Create an executable XIOS program using the GENCMD command.

5) Run the GENCCPM program under an existing CP/M-86 or Concurrent CP/M system to build the Concurrent system file. This file is an image of the Concurrent CP/M operating system.

6) Use the standard debugger, DDT-86, or Digital Research's symbolic debugger, SID-86, to place the Concurrent CP/M system file in memory for debugging.

The development time will vary depending on the implementation—development time can typically range from four to nine months.

The User Interface

Upon initial cold-start, Concurrent CP/M displays a sign-on message on the console and prompts the operator for a command. The prompt consists of a letter and an angle bracket (e.g., "A>"). The letter indicates the default disk drive (i.e., the drive where the operating system first looks for executable program files when no other drive is specified).

The command line is interpreted by the Terminal Message Processor. The TMP is a resident system process that accepts command lines from the virtual consoles and calls the Command Line Interpreter (CLI) to execute the commands.

Command lines consist of a command and an optional command tail. The command tail contains information that the command uses, such as a file specification or options. File specification components can consist of a drive specifier, a filename, a filetype, and a password. The optional drive specifier tells a program the name of the drive on which a file or group of files exists. In Figure 2-3, the four components in a file specification are illustrated.

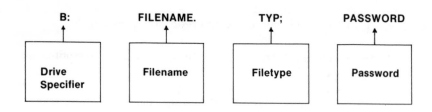

Figure 2-3 The Four Components of a File Specification.

A filename can be one to eight characters in length. The filetype is a one to three character family name of a file or group of files and always follows the filename. A password can be a one to eight character word. (Passwords are required to gain access to a protected file.) This syntax is the standard DRI operating system syntax.

The following list briefly describes all of the Concurrent CP/M commands. For a more detailed description, refer to the Concurrent CP/M Operating System User's Guide.

1) ABORT - Stops program execution on the virtual console that is specified in the command line.

2) ASM-86 - Translates 8086 assembly language source programs into a machine-readable format.

3) DATE - Displays and/or sets the date and time.

4) DDT-86 - Helps the user examine assembly language programs and interactively correct programming errors.

5) DIR - Lists the files on a specified drive or on the default drive.

6) ED - Lets the user create and alter text, data, and/or program source files.

7) ERA - Erases one or more files from a disk directory and releases the disk space occupied by the file.

8) ERAQ - Erases one or more files from a disk directory, as ERA does, but ERAQ asks the user to confirm the command for each file specified.

9) GENCCPM - Lets the programmer adjust XIOS parameters, allocate memory, and select resident system processes.

10) GENCMD - Uses ASM-86 output to produce an executable command file.

11) HELP - Displays information on how to use Concurrent CP/M commands.

12) INITDIR - Initializes a disk directory to allow date and time stamping on that disk.

13) PIP - Combines and copies files.

14) PRINTER - Shows the current default printer and lets the user change it.

15) REN - Lets the user rename a file.

16) SDIR - Displays a directory of system and nonsystem files and their attributes.

17) SET - Lets the user specify and alter certain file attributes.

18) SHOW - Displays information about system resources such as the amount of usable space on a disk.

19) SUBMIT - Sends a file of commands to Concurrent CP/M for execution.

20) SYSTAT - Displays the status of system resources (e.g., memory and queues) and shows currently running processes.

21) TYPE - Writes the contents of a text file to the screen.

22) USER - Displays the current user number or changes one user number to another.

23) VCMODE - Displays and/or sets the current background mode of the foreground virtual console.

Memory Management

Concurrent CP/M supports an extended, fixed-partition model of memory management. The Memory Module (MEM) handles all memory management system calls and is located in the invariant interface portion of the operating system. Memory is partitioned at the time of system generation into an arbitrary number of partitions, each ranging in size from IK bytes to one megabyte. Memory requests are satisfied by one or more contiguous partitions on a best-fit basis. Memory is dynamically allocated and deallocated in Concurrent CP/M. The exact method that the operating system uses to allocate and free memory is transparent to the application program and to the user.

The File System

Concurrent CP/M supports from one to sixteen logical drives. Each logical drive has two regions: a directory area and a data area. The directory area defines the files that exist on the drive and identifies the data area space that belongs to each file. The data area contains the file data defined by the directory.

The directory area consists of sixteen logically independent directories. These directories are identified by user number 0 to 15. The user number specifies the current active directories for all drives on the system. For example, the Concurrent CP/M DIR utility, without the user number option, only displays files within the directory indicated by the current user number.

The file system automatically allocates directory and data area space when a process creates or extends a file. And, when a process deletes a file, the file system returns the previously allocated space to free space. The allocation and retrieval of directory and data space are transparent to the calling process.

An eight-character filename and a three-character filetype field identify each file in a directory. Files with the same filename and filetype can reside in different user directories without conflict. Processes can also assign an eight-character password to a file to protect the file from unauthorized access.

All system calls that involve file operations specify the requested file by filename and filetype. For some system calls, multiple files can be specified by a technique called ambiguous reference. This technique uses question marks and asterisks as wild card characters to establish a pattern for the file system to match as it searches a directory.

Disk Drive and File Organization

The maximum file size supported on a drive is 32 megabytes. The maximum capacity of a drive is determined by the data block size specified for the drive in the XIOS. The data block size is the basic unit in which the BDOS allocates space to files. Using the maximum data block size of 16K, the maximum drive capacity is 512 megabytes.

Each record of a file is identified by its position in the file. This position is called the record's "random record number." If a file is created sequentially, the first record has a position of zero, while the last record has a position one less than the number of records in the file. Such a file can be read sequentially beginning at record zero, or randomly by record position. Conversely, if a file is created randomly, records are added to the file by the specified position.

The File Control Block

The File Control Block (FCB) is a system data structure that serves as an important channel for information exchange between a process and the BDOS file-access system calls. A process initializes an FCB to specify the drive location, filename and filetype fields, and other information that is required to make a file-access call. The file system also uses the FCB to maintain the current state and record position of an open file.

Before opening a file, a program must build a 36-byte data structure —the FCB. The address of the FCB is passed to the operating system to specify the file affected by the operation. (See Figure 2-4a.) The calling process must initialize the referenced FCBs before making file-access system calls.

The file system includes three special types of FCBs: the directory label, the XFCB, and the SFCB. The directory label specifies whether password support is to be activated for the drive on which the directory resides. The directory label also specifies whether file date/time stamping is to be performed. The format of the directory label is shown in Figure 2-4b. Only one directory label can exist in a drive's directory area.

The XFCB is an extended FCB that can optionally be associated with a file in the directory. If present, it contains the file's password and password mode. The format of the XFCB is shown in Figure 2-4c. An XFCB can only be created on a drive that has a directory label, and only if the directory label enables password protection.

The Concurrent CP/M file system uses a special type of directory entry called an SFCB to record date and time stamps for files. When a directory has been initialized for date and time stamping, SFCBs reside in every fourth position of the directory. Each SFCB maintains the date and time stamps for the previous three directory entries. (See Figure 2-4d.)

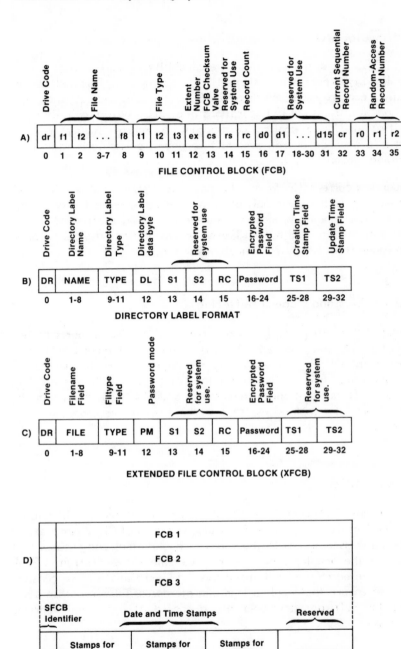

Figure 2-4 Concurrent CP/M File Control Blocks and Directory Records.

Multisector I/O

The BDOS file system provides the capability to read or write multiple 128-btye records in a single BDOS system call. This multisector facility can be visualized as a BDOS burst mode, enabling a process to complete multiple I/O operations in a single system call. By using multisector I/O, an application program can improve its performance and also enhance overall system throughput, particularly when performing sequential I/O.

Under Concurrent CP/M, the logical record size for disk I/O is 128 bytes. This is the basic unit of data transfer between the operating system and running processes. However, on disk, the record size is not restricted to 128 bytes. These records, called physical records, can range from 128 bytes to 4K bytes in size.

Hash Tables and Record Buffering

Along with multisector I/O, Concurrent CP/M also supports hashed directory access, and least-recently-used (LRU) record buffering. Concurrent CP/M uses a hashing technique to directly access directory information, eliminating the need for directory searching. Record buffers maintained in memory on a LRU scheme give the application program fast access to a working set of directory and data records.

Compatibility

Concurrent CP/M is data and file structure compatible with all Digital Research operating systems. The wide popularity of CP/M applications offers the user access to thousands of applications and ensures that most of the popular programs are available for Concurrent CP/M. Digital Research has maintained this data and file structure consistency to ensure that applications migrate across microprocessors and that the software developer has a consistent and simple porting process.

Summary

Small business machines and personal computers have become increasingly powerful, with low-cost memory storage and high-performance microprocessors. The challenge for system software developers has been to match the increasing capabilities of the hardware with the appropriate operating system software. Digital Research has met this challenge through the development of Concurrent CP/M, a single user, multitasking operating system for 8086- and 8088--based microcomputers. Being able to perform more than one task concurrently maximizes the efficiency of the user while taking full advantage of the current hardware technology.

More importantly, Concurrent CP/M has been designed to ease the porting and development time of software developers through its system architecture and its data and file structure compatibility with the Digital Research family of operating systems. This compatibility lets a software developer easily transport programs to different microprocessor systems. In addition, the same programs can function in single task, multitask, multiuser, and network environments.

References

Concurrent CP/M-86 Operating System Programmer's Reference Guide, Digital Research, Inc., 1983.

Concurrent CP/M-86 Operating System Programmer's Utilities Guide, Digital Research, Inc., 1983.

Concurrent CP/M-86 Operating System System Guide, Digital Research, Inc., 1983.

Concurrent CP/M-86 Operating System User's Guide, Digital Research, Inc., 1983.

Gary Gysin received a B.A. in Economics from the University of California, Santa Cruz, in 1982. He was the first student of Economics at UCSC to write a senior thesis. While attending school, Gary served as a consultant and developed a detailed study of sales, marketing, and finance for Side Band Engineering, Inc. Gary joined Digital Research in 1982 as a technical support representative in the Customer Support Department. He currently is the product line manager for Concurrent CP/M in the Product Marketing Group at Digital Research. Gary's hobbies include playing all sports; he is a member of the Professional Beach Volleyball Association Circuit.

Chapter 3

THE MS-DOS OPERATING SYSTEM

Microsoft's Disk Operating System
for 16-Bit Microcomputers

Bharat Sastri
Epson America, Inc.

3

Microsoft's MS-DOS operating system is a general purpose disk operating system designed for the 16-bit microprocessor environment. This operating system provides a single user, single task interactive environment that facilitates diverse applications from word processing to program development.

The MS-DOS system is currently designed for use with the Intel 8086/8088 microprocessor family. While the operating system itself requires 32K bytes of memory, practical usage requires at least 64K bytes for flexible diskette systems and 128K bytes for hard disk systems.

Many hardware manufacturers offer MS-DOS 2.0 as an option on their machines. This action has led to the availability of a large pool of applications and systems software that is largely portable between different hardware.

Operating System Overview

There are three primary building blocks that are required for the implementation or customization of the MS-DOS system on a specific vendor's hardware. These blocks or modules are:

1) The Disk Operating System (DOS).

2) The Basic Input Output Section (BIOS).

3) The Command Processor (COMMAND).

The DOS module is hardware-independent and is provided by Microsoft. The DOS implements a hierarchical disk file system and provides a user interface through a set of 72 separate system primitives or system functions. Application programs interface with the DOS in a standard manner and are thus portable between different machines running the same version of MS-DOS.

The BIOS module is the hardware-dependent module. This module provides the link between the DOS module and the particular hardware on which the operating system is implemented.

The BIOS consists of two components: the ROM resident code that provides the lowest level of control over the hardware and the installable device drivers that provide a higher level of abstraction from the actual hardware. These components are discussed in more detail later in the chapter.

The COMMAND module is also hardware-independent and is provided by Microsoft. This module is the link between the console user and the operating system (embodied in the DOS module). The COMMAND module is memory-resident and contains a host of directive functions (commands) known as the "internal commands." An example of an internal command is DIR—the directive that displays the directory of a disk.

In addition to these modules, the implementation of the operating system requires the writing of several utilities that perform various specialized tasks such as formatting and copying disks. Utilities and other special commands, which are implemented to complement the operating system software, are in essence application programs that make use of operating system facilities through the standard DOS interface.

The DOS Module

As mentioned earlier, the DOS module provides a hardware-independent file system implementation. In addition, the DOS also implements other system functions (e.g., memory allocation and deallocation).

The MS-DOS operating system provides two types of interfaces to the DOS module: interrupts and function requests. Interrupts 28H through 40H are reserved by the system. User programs may issue interrupts 20H, 21H, 25H, 26H and 27H only. Table 3-1 lists the interrupts in numeric order.

Function requests are invoked by loading a function number into a designated register and causing interrupt 21H. A list of DOS functions is provided in Table 3-2.

The majority of the DOS function requests in Table 3-2 require parameters that must be passed to the DOS. There are three prescribed methods of invoking these functions. The most commonly-used method requires application programs to set up the parameters in the appropriate processor registers, set the desired function number in register AH, and call the reserved software interrupt number 21H.

The BIOS

The BIOS contains the code that insulates the DOS module from the hardware. The BIOS, in general, is composed of two parts: a ROM-resident module that provides the lowest level of code necessary to manipulate the various VLSI chips and a RAM-based module that provides the link between the DOS and the ROM-based routines.

The first BIOS module is entirely ROM based and is therefore referred to as the ROM BIOS. The ROM BIOS is implemented as a group of interrupt service routines that support the system hardware. Each interrupt service routine may be invoked by executing the 8086/8088 INT instruction. Some of the interrupt routines require parameters in order to execute correctly. All parameters are passed

Interrupt Number	Description
20H	Program terminate.
21H	Function request.
22H	Terminate address.
23H	Control-C exit address.
24H	Fatal error abort address.
25H	Absolute disk read.
26H	Absolute disk write.
27H	Terminate but stay resident.
28H-40H	Reserved.

Table 3-1 MS-DOS 2.0 Interrupts.

Function Number	Action
00H	Terminate program.
01H	Read keyboard and echo.
02H	Display character.
03H	Auxiliary input.
04H	Auxiliary output.
05H	Print character.
06H	Direct console I/O.
07H	Direct console input.
08H	Read keyboard.
09H	Display string.
0AH	Buffered keyboard input.
0BH	Check keyboard status.
0CH	Flush buffer, read keyboard.
0DH	Disk reset.
0EH	Select disk.
0FH	Open file.
10H	Close file.
11H	Search for first entry.
12H	Search for next entry.
13H	Delete file.
14H	Sequential read.
15H	Sequential write.
16H	Create file.
17H	Rename file.
19H	Current disk.
1AH	Set disk transfer address.
21H	Random read.
22H	Random write.
23H	File size.
24H	Set relative record.
25H	Set vector.
27H	Random block read.
28H	Random block write.
29H	Parse filename.
2AH	Get date.
2BH	Set date.

Table 3-2 MS-DOS 2.0 Function Requests.

Function Number	Action
2CH	Get time.
2DH	Set time.
2EH	Set/reset verify flag.
2FH	Get disk transfer address.
30H	Get DOS version number.
31H	Keep process.
33H	Control-C check.
35H	Get interrupt vector.
36H	Get disk free space.
38H	Return country dependent information.
39H	Create subdirectory.
3AH	Remove a directory entry.
3BH	Change current directory.
3CH	Create a file.
3DH	Open a file.
3EH	Close a file.
3FH	Read from a file/device.
40H	Write to a file/device.
41H	Delete a directory.
42H	Move a file pointer.
43H	Change attributes.
44H	I/O control for devices.
45H	Duplicate a file/handle.
46H	Force a duplicate of a handle.
47H	Return text of current directory.
48H	Allocate memory.
49H	Free allocated memory.
4AH	Modify allocated memory blocks.
4BH	Load and execute a program.
4CH	Terminate a process.
4DH	Retrieve and return code of child.
4EH	Find match file.
4FH	Step through directory, matching files.
54H	Return current setting of verify.
56H	Move a directory entry.
57H	Get/set date/time of file.

Table 3-2 (continued) MS-DOS 2.0 Function Requests.

in processor registers. Parameters and/or status information are also returned in processor registers.

The second part of the BIOS module is implemented as a group of logical device driver routines that provide the bridge between the DOS and the physical devices they access. Table 3-3 contains a list of the valid logical devices, their physical images, and the device drivers that provide the link between the two.

A device driver is a binary file that contains the code necessary to manipulate the hardware. A device driver has a well-defined structure under MS-DOS. A special header at the beginning of the file identifies the code as a device driver. The header also defines the entry points for the device driver routines and the attributes of the device.

There are two types of device drivers: character device drivers and block device drivers. Character devices are designed to perform serial character input and output. Examples of character devices are the console, the printer, and the serial I/O port. Each character device has a name associated with it. Devices with identical functions but different names may utilize the same driver routines by providing different headers—even though the entry points to the routines are the same. For example, both the COM: device and the AUX: device manipulate the same hardware (i.e., the serial communications hardware). Although both devices have different headers, the headers map to the same service routines.

Logical Device	Function	Physical Device	Device Driver
CON:	Console I/O	CRT, Keyboard	CONSOLE
AUX:	Serial I/O	RS-232-C Device	AUXILIARY
PRN:	Parallel I/O	Printers	PRINTER
TIM:	Time of Day	Clock	CLOCK
DSK:	Disk R/W	Disk Drives	DISK
COM1:	Serial I/O	RS-232-C Device	AUXILIARY
LPT1:	Parallel I/O	Printers	PRINTER

Table 3-3 BIOS Function and Device Driver Map.

Block devices, on the other hand, may perform random input and output in multibyte "blocks." Disk drives are the typical block devices in any system. Thus, the block size is usually the size of one physical sector on the disk. Unlike character devices, block devices do not have names and may not be opened directly for input and output. Block devices are identified by the drive letters A:, B:, C:, etc.

A single driver may be responsible for one or several drives. For example, if one disk driver can control up to four disk drives, the driver is said to control four "units" (numbered 0, 1, 2, and 3) identified by A:, B:, C:, and D:. The next disk driver controls the units with identifiers starting at E:, and so on. The theoretical limit is 64 block device units. However, only the first 26 units are identified by the letters of the alphabet.

The Device Header

The primary BIOS data structure is the device header, which is mandatory for every device. The device drivers are implemented as a linked list of device headers. Each device header points to the next device header in the list. The last device is identified by "-1" in its pointer field. The exact structure is shown in Figure 3-1.

Pointer to next device
Attributes
Strategy
Interrupt
Name

Figure 3-1 The Device Driver Header.

The pointer field is a double word field that points to the next driver in the system list at the time the driver is loaded. If the current driver is the last one in the list, the offset portion of the pointer is set equal to "-1".

The attribute field is a word field used to identify the device as either a character or a block device. Each bit in the field signifies the presence or absence of a specific attribute of that driver. Some of the important attributes are:

1) Whether the device is a character device or a block device.

2) Whether the device is the current standard input and standard output for the system. The standard input and standard output in the system are defined as the default devices for console input and output (normally the CON: device).

3) Whether the device is the NUL device. The NUL device is actually a garbage bin to which unwanted output is sent. The NUL device cannot be reassigned.

4) Whether the device is the current clock device.

5) Whether a disk device is recorded in an IBM PC format. This information is used to control the execution of certain disk driver commands.

The strategy and interrupt fields are pointers to the entry points of the strategy and interrupt routines, respectively, for that device.

The name field is an 8-byte field that contains the name of a character device or the number of units for a block device.

The Request Header

The second important data structure is the request header. The request header is a fixed-length header followed by data pertinent to the operation to be performed.

When DOS calls a device driver to perform a function, it makes a call to the strategy routine of that driver and passes a pointer to the request header. A typical request header is shown in Figure 3-2.

The unit code field defines the device unit to which the request applies. The command code field identifies the command to be executed. There are thirteen valid commands such as Init, Input, Input Status, Output, and Output Status.

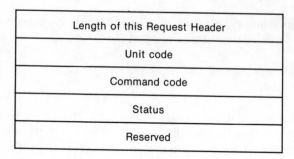

| Length of this Request Header |
| Unit code |
| Command code |
| Status |
| Reserved |

Figure 3-2 The Request Header.

The status word of the request header reflects the result of the request. On entry to the device driver, the status is 0; the status is
set to a result value by the driver. Errors that are reported through
the status word include write protect violations, unknown units, seek
errors, etc.

Installable Device Drivers

In addition to the default device drivers, MS-DOS provides a facility
to install additional device drivers dynamically at boot time. At bootstrap time, the MS-DOS operating system checks for the existence of
a file called CONFIG.SYS, which contains a list of device drivers to
be installed dynamically. Since MS-DOS always processes installable
drivers prior to the default device drivers, it is easy to install a
new console device by simply naming it CON and setting the standard
input and output bits in the attribute word. The scanning of the device driver list terminates at the first match and hence the installable driver overrides the default.

The Command Processor

The COMMAND processor module controls the MS-DOS human-
machine interface. It processes commands that are entered by the
user and invokes the appropriate programs.

There are two types of commands that exist under MS-DOS: internal
or "built-in" commands and external or "transient" commands. Internal

commands are an integral part of the COMMAND processor and are always available in memory as long as the COMMAND module was loaded
during the system bootstrap. Transient commands, on the other hand,
are resident on disk and are loaded into memory by the COMMAND
module when required. Some transient commands, however, have the
ability to remain memory-resident after they are loaded. Some of the
most commonly-used commands are listed in Table 3-4.

The Command Interface

The normal system prompt is the default drive letter followed by
">" in the form of "A>". This sequence may be altered by a
system command called PROMPT.

Commands and parameters may be entered in both upper and lower
case. The parameters must be separated by a delimiter such as a space,
semicolon, comma, etc. Commands become effective only after a
carriage return is entered.

When command execution is complete, the prompt reappears. Any error
is reported on the screen by means of a message; the absence of an
error message signifies successful command completion.

Command	Type	Description
DIR	Internal	Displays a disk directory.
DEL	Internal	Deletes a file from a directory.
COPY	Internal	Duplicates a file.
TYPE	Internal	Prints a file to the screen.
MKDIR	Internal	Creates a new directory.
RMDIR	Internal	Removes a directory.
CHDIR	Internal	Changes present directory.
FORMAT	External	Formats a flexible diskette.
DISKCOPY	External	Duplicates a flexible diskette.
MORE	External	Outputs to console by pages.
PRINT	External	Starts background printing.

Table 3-4 Commonly Used MS-DOS Commands.

Commands may be aborted by entering control-C during execution. It is also possible to suspend large output displays (by entering control-S) and restart the display (by entering control-Q). These inputs must be supplied from the keyboard.

The command processor recognizes all ASCII characters. The characters * and ? are treated as wild cards for filenames. However, the characters <,>,| have special meaning and will be described later in the section on special features.

In addition, the command processor can also execute commands in a batch mode. This facility permits automatic execution of programs.

The File System

The MS-DOS operating system implements a hierarchical file system. When a diskette is created, a single directory is placed on it. This directory is called the system or root directory. The directory's location and the number of entries in the directory are functions of the disk media.

In addition to containing filenames, the root directory contains the names of other directories. These directories, called subdirectories, are treated like ordinary files and hence do not suffer from the size restrictions of the root directory. In fact, subdirectory size is limited only by the available disk space. Subdirectories may themselves contain other subdirectories.

All filenames and subdirectory names have the same format—a one to eight character name followed by a period and an optional three character extension. For example, "MYFILE.DOC" is a valid name.

The MS-DOS operating system supports the concept of a "current directory," which is analogous to the current drive. The current directory is defined as the directory that DOS will search for a file if no directory is specified. A user may change the current directory by invoking the CHDIR command.

The concept of a "pathname" is closely connected to the concept of a hierarchical file system. To create, to search for, or to alter a file, DOS needs three coordinates: the drive, the name of the file, and the name of the directory in which the file resides. The "pathname" consists of a series of directory names separated by backslashes ("\"). If the file name is included in the pathname, it must be separated from the last directory name by a backslash. If a pathname begins with a backslash, DOS starts its search from the root directory; otherwise the search originates at the current directory.

DOS Disk Allocation

MS-DOS supports several types of storage media including flexible diskettes and hard disks. Disks may be formatted in a number of different formats but most personal computers use either 8 or 9 sectors per track. Obvious differences in the storage space affect the size of the reserved space and the data space available. Figure 3-3 illustrates a typical disk layout.

MS-DOS disks are usually created with a sector size of 512 bytes. All space allocation is performed dynamically and is not preallocated. Space is allocated in units called "clusters;" one cluster is allocated at a time. A cluster is a collection of one or more contiguous sectors on the disk. All clusters for a file are chained together in a data structure called the File Allocation Table or FAT.

Clusters are arranged to minimize head travel on multisided media. All of the space on a cylinder must be allocated prior to moving to the next cylinder. This goal is achieved by allocating sequential sectors on the lowest number head, followed by sectors of the next higher number head, and so on until all space on a cylinder is allocated.

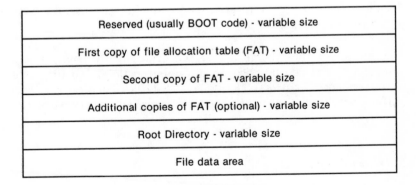

Figure 3-3 Disk Layout.

Files are not written on the disk in one continous block; instead, the data space is allocated one cluster at a time, skipping clusters that are already allocated. The command CHKDSK is used to determine how many contiguous disk areas are allocated to a file. Greater fragmentation leads to poorer performance. To reduce the number of fragments in a file, the file must be copied to a new disk using the COPY command.

A typical 5¼-inch 40 track/inch double-sided diskette formatted with 9 sectors per track has 360K bytes of data space. The root directory size is 112 entries and the cluster size is 2 sectors.

Data required to allow different manufacturers to read each other's media is stored on the boot track of the media. The data permits the reconstruction of a data structure called the BIOS Parameter Block (BPB) for a particular media. The data describes parameters such as the sector size, the number of FATs, the number of root directories, etc. The BPB is used by the block device drivers to access the physical disk device.

The file system supports all standard operations such as open, close, create, delete, and supports both sequential and random file access. File access protection is implemented in the sense that a file may be declared to be a "system" file or a "read-only" file. System files are invisible to users and read-only files cannot be overwritten.

MS-DOS does not require an application to construct any special control blocks before opening or creating files. Instead, an ASCII string consisting of the drive, the pathname, and the filename may be passed to the DOS. The DOS locates an existing file or creates a new file and returns a 16-bit binary value referred to as the file "handle." All subsequent references to the file can use the handle as the file identifier.

The number of files that MS-DOS can open simultaneously is eight (by default) and can be changed at bootstrap time. The file system also uses cache buffers. Normally, MS-DOS allocates two cache buffers, but the number may be changed dynamically at bootstrap time.

Software Tools

MS-DOS provides the software tools required to develop and debug assembly language programs. These tools are the line text editor

(EDLIN), the macroassembler (MASM), the linker (LINK), and the debugger (DEBUG).

EDLIN is used to create source files and delete, edit, insert, and display lines. The editor can also operate on text within one or more lines.

MASM is a macroassembler that creates non-executable object files from source programs.

LINK is used to combine object modules and create relocatable executable files from the output of MASM. The output of the linker is a file with an extension of ".EXE".

The DEBUG program provides a controlled environment for the testing and development of a program. The debugger has several features such as the ability to set breakpoints and load, alter, or display memory. DEBUG has a set of commands that allow in-line assembly and disassembly of code.

Special System Features

Programs executing under the MS-DOS operating system can receive input from a source other than the keyboard (the standard input device) or direct output to a device other than the console (the standard output device). This capability is called I/O redirection. The special characters that identify I/O redirection to the command processor are "<", ">", and ">>". For example, ">PROG.LOG" on the command line directs the output to the file PROG.LOG. ">>PROG.LOG" appends the program output to the file PROG.LOG. In a similar manner, "<SCRIPT" dictates that keyboard input is to be read from the file SCRIPT.

Another important MS-DOS feature is the ability to create "pipes." A pipe allows the screen output of one program to be used as the keyboard input of the next program. The two programs to be piped together are separated by the vertical bar ("|") on the command line (e.g., "PROGRAM1 | PROGRAM2").

The MS-DOS system also allows the operating environment to be modified at bootstrap time. The parameters that can be changed are the number of disk buffers, the device drivers, the number of files that can be opened for simultaneous access, and even the command processor. To change the operating environment, the user creates a file called CONFIG.SYS in the root directory. CONFIG.SYS contains text information that sets values for all new parameters. For example, "DEVICE=NEWCON.COM" will cause NEWCON to be installed as a device driver.

Summary

The MS-DOS operating system has found favor with a wide spectrum of personal computer manufacturers. Because of this fact, a large number of applications programs are available under the MS-DOS system. In addition, the machine-independent implementation of the operating system ensures software portability between machines executing MS-DOS on 8086 family processors.

References

IBM PC-DOS 2.0 Manual, IBM Corporation.

IBM PC Technical Reference Manual, IBM Corporation.

Microsoft MS-DOS 2.0 Programmers Reference, Microsoft, Inc.

Microsoft MS-DOS 2.0 Users Reference, Microsoft, Inc.

Bharat Sastri is currently manager of operating systems and languages at the Advanced Products Division of Epson America, Inc. Prior to joining Epson, he was the software project manager for the Osborne PC product. Bharat was also involved in networking and communications software at Zilog, Inc. He has graduate degrees in Computer Science and Electrical Engineering from the Indian Institute of Science, Bangalore, India.

Chapter 4

THE MSP OPERATING SYSTEM

*A Real-time Solution for Development
and Embedded Applications*

Robert D. Grappel
Hemenway Corporation

4

The Hemenway Corporation MSP (Multitasking System Program) operating system combines the essential ingredients needed for both development and execution of real-time applications. MSP systems can be configured "a la carte" to include only those features required by a particular application. MSP configurations range from embedded ROM-based systems to complete development stations.

MSP systems are available for the 68000 and Z8002 processors. Ranging in size from approximately 8K bytes to 24K bytes (depending on the configuration), MSP is compact and efficient. MSP systems are fully ROMable. In addition, a wide variety of hardware can be accommodated since all the hardware dependencies are separated into linkable "device drivers."

The MSP systems present the user with a hierarchical structure as illustrated in Figure 4-1. At the center of this structure is the actual hardware—including the processor, memory, I/O devices, mass storage, and any special-purpose components needed for the application. Each successive layer of MSP wraps the lower layer with a further level of functionality, thereby creating an increasingly powerful virtual machine. However, unlike many operating systems in which the application can address only the outermost layer, MSP gives the user access to all layers of the system through over 70 system calls.

The Kernel

Six optimized kernel routines supply the key services needed in a real-time multitasking system for mutual exclusion and task synchronization. The MSP kernel uses the **monitor** concept introduced by C.A.R. Hoare and elaborated by P.B. Hansen to provide task synchronization and mutual exclusion. In a monitor, all the critical sections of code for a particular set of shared data are collected into one module. Each critical section becomes an entry point to the monitor. Whenever one of the entries is invoked, exclusive access to the shared

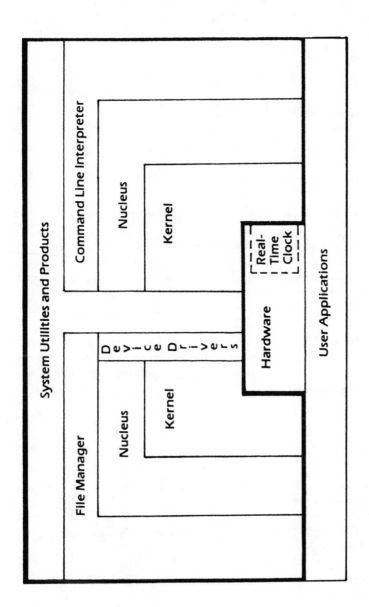

Figure 4-1 The Hierarchical Structure of the MSP Operating System.

data is automatically provided. Thus, enforcement of mutual exclusion is implicit—a programmer need only invoke the appropriate entry. Monitors are the fundamental synchronization construct in MSP and are used to build other synchronization primitives such as mailbox mechanisms. Five monitor primitives provide an application with direct control over tasks and resources:

1) Entermon - Enter a critical section.

2) Exitmon - Leave a critical section.

3) Wait - Block a task awaiting a resource.

4) Signal - Run a blocked task.

5) Unblock - Place a blocked task on the ready queue.

In addition, a real-time clock interrupt handler in the kernel provides a second means of task control. A check of the task queue is performed at each clock "tick," preventing any task from monopolizing the system. Moreover, the task queue is prioritized, with tasks of equal priority running in a round-robin fashion.

One significant feature of the monitor design is the ease with which it may be extended to support multiprocessor hardware. All the necessary extensions can be embedded in the kernel; the rest of MSP need not change at all.

MSP Task Control

A set of system calls in the MSP kernel provides for dynamic task control. These include:

1) GETPCB - Start a task by acquiring a Process Control Block (PCB).

2) GIVPCB - Kill a task by relinquishing the PCB to the system.

3) GSTAT - Get the current state of a task.

4) SETPRI - Change the priority of a task.

5) DELAY - Cause a task to stop running for a given period.

6) WAKEUP - Cause a delayed task to resume running.

Tasks may be created and controlled in response to events. There is no need to **sysgen** tasks into the system; tasks can be started and controlled by any application program. Moreover, task priorities may be altered based on real-time system constraints.

Intertask Communication

The monitor primitives provide a very efficient control mechanism for tasks and resources, but they do not directly provide an intertask message-passing facility. MSP adds a set of **mailbox** system calls that address this common multitasking requirement. Any pair of tasks in the system can use MSP mailboxes to exchange variable-length messages. Also, tasks can inquire about the availability of messages directed to them and can determine the identity of the sending task. The mailbox system calls are:

1) GETBOX - Acquire the use of a mailbox.

2) GIVBOX - Relinquish the use of a mailbox.

3) MSTAT - Determine the status of a mailbox.

4) SEND - Send a message to another task.

5) RECVE - Receive a message from another task.

6) CKMAIL - Inquire about mail for a task.

7) CKINAM - Check the identity of a sending task.

Memory Management

MSP also provides memory management facilities. Memory within an MSP system is divided into a **transient** space and a **managed** space. The transient space allows absolute programs (e.g., programs stored in ROM) to be used. The managed space allows applications to acquire blocks of memory for use and to subsequently release the blocks back to the system. The development configuration dynamically relocates programs or allows programs to be fixed into the transient space. Memory management is done in 2K-byte blocks. The management algorithm is performed in software—no MMU hardware is required.

MSP can manage the entire addressing range of the system processor. In addition, code and data areas can be loaded into separate memory blocks.

I/O Support

The nucleus (see Figure 4-1) surrounds the kernel with I/O support. MSP provides application programs with several levels of I/O system calls. The most basic I/O system call is IOHDLR. IOHDLR is a device-independent service that provides buffered I/O for any named device in the system. IOHDLR includes the necessary monitor calls to control task access to I/O devices. Standard MSP devices include:

1)   CON - Main console.

2)   LPT - Line printer.

3)   TTY - Alternate console (external serial line).

4)   DSK - Mass storage (flexible diskettes, hard disks, etc.)

5)   NUL - "Bit-bucket."

MSP also supports a set of user-definable devices. System calls SETDEV and RESDEV allow a user to add special-purpose device drivers to the system. These drivers enjoy the same overall structure and protection afforded to the standard device drivers. Note that it is not necessary to regenerate the system to add or delete drivers.

Device drivers in MSP are interrupt driven. Therefore, MSP tasks do not waste processor time waiting for I/O devices. In addition, type-ahead is supported for the CON and TTY devices.

Nucleus System Calls

The nucleus also contains routines that are very useful in applications. Many of these are made available to the user as system calls. The most basic set of these system calls are:

1)   PRTMSG - Print a line on the console.

2)   PRTERR - Print a standard error message on the console.

3)   GTCMD - Read a line from the console (or from a SUBMIT file).

4)   NXTOK - Parse a text line into lexigraphical tokens.

5)   FMTFCB - Parse, error check, and reformat a file specification.

6)   LOADB - Load a binary file into memory.

7)   LOADR - Relocate and load a task image.

Use of GTCMD lets any application receive commands from an active SUBMIT file. Parameter substitution is performed automatically by MSP. If there is no active SUBMIT file, GTCMD prompts and accepts input from the console. GTCMD automatically expands tabs and responds to console SET values. PRTERR outputs a standardized error message for any type of MSP I/O. NXTOK parses a line of text into a set of tokens. (While NXTOK is usually used to parse command lines, it may also be used to parse text within an application program.) The following tokens can be isolated by NXTOK:

1)   Word - An alphanumeric string. NXTOK returns the string's address and length.

2)   Number - A decimal or hexadecimal integer. NXTOK returns the binary value.

3)   Delimiter - A standard delimiter, such as a comma, a period, a carriage return, etc.).

4)   Wild card - A word containing "*" or "?".

NXTOK is very useful to any application program that must accept text commands. Finally, FMTFCB is a high-level system call that parses a file specification and reformats the specification as required by MSP.

OS/ENGINE

The minimal configuration of MSP described in the preceding sections can be used to solve a large class of real-time problems. This MSP configuration forms a fully-functional execution vehicle for ROM-based embedded applications. Stripped down to this level, MSP becomes OS/ENGINE. As a proper subset of MSP, OS/ENGINE applications can be developed and tested under MSP. The system calls and structures of OS/ENGINE match those of MSP. OS/ENGINE, with drivers for CON, TTY, and LPT devices, requires less than 8K bytes.

Debugging a real-time application on the target hardware can be difficult. Conventional debugging techniques are often useless for isolating and solving multitask problems. Therefore, OS/ENGINE includes a debugger that may be used to probe the hardware and software state of the machine without disrupting the application tasks. OS/ENGINE's debugger is similar to the task debugger available on the development configuration of MSP. Access to machine registers, memory, and I/O devices is provided.

The debugger runs as a task under OS/ENGINE. If required, a user may "kill" the debugger and allow the application tasks to completely control the machine. Also, a target configuration of OS/ENGINE is available without the debugger.

The FILE System

The File Manager layer of MSP gives the user control over a powerful and flexible file system. The DSK device is treated as a set of **logical** drives. Each drive consists of N logical sectors (numbered 0 through N-1). All considerations of device-specific parameters, such as track/sector/cylinder mapping and interleave factors, are left to the DSK device driver. Any combination of drives, including flexible diskettes (single/double-sided, single/double-density), hard disks, etc., can be used. The MSP interface to the DSK driver has only three entries.

    1)   INTDK - Initialize the drives and configure DSK tables.

    2)   RDSEC - Read a logical sector.

    3)   WTSEC - Write a logical sector.

Each logical drive has a file directory. A directory entry for a file contains the file name, the extension, the file type, the access code, the file size, and a time-stamp. Wild card directory searches permit selection of file classes based on name or extension. In addition, system calls are provided to address and modify directories.

The basic MSP file (sequential file) consists of a linked-list of logical sectors. The list is constructed during disk initialization and the list is maintained by MSP system calls. The linked-list structure provides fast, dynamic control of variable-length files. In addition, sequential file I/O system calls provide character and line protocols. Text files automatically compress runs of blanks to single characters when writing and expand them back to blanks when reading. Moreover, mutual exclusion monitors prevent conflicts when several tasks try to access the same directory. Finally, MSP allows multiple tasks to read the same file simultaneously.

In addition to sequential files, MSP also supports an area on each logical drive in which contiguous file allocation and deallocation is performed. The MSP system calls for contiguous files allow applications to load and store data more rapidly than is possible with sequential files. Single system calls allow tasks to read or write large amounts of data in a single operation.

The contiguous area supports random-access files. A random-access file is defined as a set of N fixed-length records. Positioning of a random-access file to any arbitrary record requires only a single disk access. System calls to read or write a file record are provided. Moreover, records may be updated in place.

Since reclaiming space after a contiguous or random-access file has been deleted is a time-consuming operation, this reclamation is performed by the system task, COMPRESS, which may be run as time permits. COMPRESS runs in the background, allowing other tasks to continue executing.

The Human Interface

The user of MSP interacts most directly with the layer called the Command Line Interpreter (CLI). The CLI is actually a task running under control of the kernel. (In OS/ENGINE the debugger takes the place of the CLI task.) CLI accepts commands from the console or from a batch file (SUBMIT command). CLI carries out commands by dispatching them to lower level routines, by loading and executing transient commands from disk, or by loading task images. CLI uses a straightforward, consistent syntax typical of that used on mini-computers.

Table 4-1 gives the command set mnemonics for MSP/68000. (The Z8002 set is similar.) Note that there are CLI commands corresponding to some of the system calls described previously:

Command Mnemonic	Equivalent System Call
RUN	GETPCB
KILL	GIVPCB
TASKS	GSTAT
SUSPEND	DELAY
RESUME	WAKEUP
PRIOR	SETPRI

The CLI allows users to abbreviate commands to their first three characters. Transient programs are run by simply using their file specification as a command. (Transient programs are executed as extensions of the CLI task.) Only the PIP and the INIT commands are transients; the rest of the commands are resident in the CLI. The following paragraphs describe some of the most powerful CLI commands.

PIP (Peripheral Interchange Program) is a workhorse data transfer command. PIP transfers information from any device or file to another device or file. This command can be used to copy complete disks or individual files. In addition, files may be concatenated with PIP. PIP can also be used to create text files, to print files, and to reformat files. Moreover, PIP can convert MSP's internal binary format to hexadecimal (ASCII) format and back again. This feature is useful when transfering files between different systems. For example, coupled with the TTY device's type-ahead buffer, the PIP command,

    PIP MYFILE.IN=TTY

will build MYFILE from the serial port at transfer rates up to 9600 baud—handshaking protocols are not needed.

The LINK command allows a user to create a system boot file from any binary file on a disk. This facilitates system modifications and turn-key applications. MSP can also access a batch file on start-up.

This file can be used to initially configure an application by automatically entering a set of predefined CLI commands. The SUBMIT
command also uses a file as a source of CLI commands for the system.
In addition, SUBMIT supports a macro-like facility that allows a user

ASSIGN	Assigns a logical device name to a physical device.
CCONT	Creates a contiguous file.
CRAND	Creates a random file.
DELETE	Removes a file from the disk.
DENSITY	Changes the density parameters of a specified disk.
DIR	Prints the directory of the specified disk drive.
EXIT	Passes control to the hardware debug monitor.
INIT	Initializes the specified diskette.
JUMP	Passes control to an absolute address.
KILL	Removes a task from the system.
LINK	Makes a diskette bootable.
LOAD	Loads a binary program.
PIP	Loads and executes the Peripheral Interchange Program.
PRIOR	Changes the priority of a task
RENAME	Changes the name of a disk file.
RESUME	Resumes a task.
RUN	Loads and starts a task.
SAVE	Saves an area of memory as a binary file.
SECURE	Sets a file's access codes.
SET	Changes the console or line printer parameters.
STATUS	Lists the present device assignments.
SUBMIT	Executes commands from a command file.
SUSPEND	Suspends a task.
TASK	Displays status of all tasks in system.
TIME	Displays and sets the real-time clock.

Table 4-1 MSP Command Summary.

to specify parameters on the command line. SUBMIT inserts these parameters into the proper locations within the file's commands before passing the commands to CLI.

CLI commands that affect tasks use alphanumeric names to refer to the appropriate tasks. The task name is usually the file name of the task image. The mapping from task name to the internal PCB address is done automatically in CLI. Also, like files, tasks are time-stamped.

Error Reporting

Since the user has the most contact with CLI, many human interface errors are detected at this level. CLI responds to erroneous commands with English messages. For instance, I/O errors report the name of the device in use. In addition, most errors permit a retry of the command.

Run-time errors are especially hard to handle in a multitask environment. MSP builds on the error trapping inherent in the processor and in the system hardware. Traps such as "invalid address," "divide by zero," etc., are handled by MSP. When an error is detected, MSP prints a debug dump that includes the name of the task that caused the error, the error type, and the register contents at the time of the error. In addition, the system will close any currently open files and reinitialize itself.

Operation Without CLI

As was the case with OS/ENGINE's debugger task, MSP can run without an active CLI task. If desired, CLI can be used to set up the system for an application. The user can subsequently KILL or SUSPEND the CLI task. This action leaves the user's applications in control of the machine. Running without CLI lets the user test applications that are destined for OS/ENGINE.

MSP's Utilities and Products

The outer shell of MSP includes a large number of utilities and programs that allow MSP to support software development. For example, a text editor and a macro-assembler run under MSP. (The 68000 assembler is source-compatible with Motorola's assembly language syntax, while the Z8002 assembler follows Zilog's syntax.) Both the editor and assembler are tasks—a user can edit one file while assembling another. The assemblers feature conditional assembly and cross-reference generation.

MSP supports a PLMH language compiler for both the 68000 and the Z8002 processors. The PL/M language was developed by Intel and the MSP compilers are source compatible with Intel's PL/M-80 language. PLMH is a systems programming language. It is a fully structured high-level language that permits reentrant procedures, interrupt handling, pointer manipulation, etc. In addition, libraries to interface PLMH to all MSP system calls are provided.

MSP/68000 supports an extended BASIC interpreter whose primary features are execution speed and source compatibility with 8-bit BASIC dialects. HC-BASIC supports 16- and 32-bit integers, 32- and 64-bit reals, and variable-length character strings. Output formatting via the PRINT USING statement, as well as full random-access and sequential file capabilities are also included. HC-BASIC can call assembly language routines and pass any number of parameters (by address or value). HC-BASIC is extensible—up to 255 new keywords can be added.

MSP/68000 also supports a Pascal compiler. This compiler produces either P-code (for interpretation) or native code (for direct execution). Separate compilation, double-precision reals, extensive optimization, and libraries to interface Pascal programs to all MSP system calls are provided.

MSP includes a linker and a librarian that can combine object modules from assemblers or compilers. The MSP locater program binds a linked program to absolute addresses, while the MSP task-builder program converts a program into task-image form.

A task debugger (similar to the debugger in OS/ENGINE) is supplied as a linkable module. The debugger is linked into the task to be tested and does not affect other tasks in the system. The debugger allows a user to display and alter the contents of processor registers and memory locations. In addition, users can set breakpoints in the task being debugged. Also, a set of relocation registers makes it easy to reference locations in blocks of memory acquired through the memory management functions of MSP.

A simple print-spooler task is also provided with MSP as an example of how to write an MSP task. Source code of the spooler (in assembly language) may be found in the MSP Advanced User's Guide.

Two additional disk utilities depend on the capabilities of the disk controller hardware. The FORMAT utility formats and initializes disks. FORMAT can handle single- and double-density, as well as single- and double-sided flexible diskettes. The FCOPY utility performs fast disk copies. FCOPY reads and writes entire disk tracks and can duplicate a flexible diskette in about 45 seconds. (For comparison, PIP requires several minutes to copy the same amount of data.)

The SPLIT utility divides a binary file into high and low bytes in preparation for PROM programming. MIKSPLIT downloads the program into a PROM programmer.

Finally, floating-point math and scientific function packages are available for both single-precision (32-bit) and double-precision (64-bit) computations. The floating point operations include basic math, trigonometric functions, logarithms, exponentials, and format conversions.

Summary

Hemenway Corporation's MSP operating system is a configurable and extensible system that covers the spectrum from embedded applications to development systems. Starting from a small but efficient kernel, MSP grows in power as operating system layers are added. For each user, MSP may be customized to meet his/her specific needs and challenges.

References

MSP Operating System User Guide, Hemenway Corporation, 1981.

MSP Operating System Advanced User Guide, Hemenway Corporation, 1981.

MSP/68000 Nucleus User Guide, Hemenway Corporation, 1983.

MSP/68000 File Manager User Guide, Hemenway Corporation, 1983.

MSP/68000 System Configuration Guide, Hemenway Corporation, 1982.

MSP Debugger Reference Manual, Hemenway Corporation, 1982.

MSP Link, Locate, Library Manager User Guide, Hemenway Corporation, 1982.

Robert D. Grappel is currently vice-president at Hemenway Corporation. He previously worked at MIT's Lincoln Laboratory as a senior research staff member. He has M.S. and B.S. degrees in Physics and Computer Science.

Chapter 5

THE PICK OPERATING SYSTEM

*A Multiuser, Virtual Memory Data Base
Management System*

Jonathan E. Sisk
JES & Associates, Inc.

William W. Walsh
Kenneth O. All
PICK SYSTEMS

5

The PICK operating system is a multiuser, virtual memory database management system that provides consistent operational characteristics on a wide range of micro, mini, super-mini, and mainframe computers. The system's first microprocessor implementation occurred in 1982 on Digital Equipment Corporation's LSI-11. The PICK operating system is now also available on the Zilog Z8000, the Motorola 68000, and the Intel 8086/8088 microprocessors.

This operating system is not available to end users directly from PICK SYSTEMS; rather, PICK SYSTEMS relies on distribution through licensees. These licensees are typically OEMs, system integrators, or VARs, and they serve both vertical and territorial end user markets through direct sales representatives, independent sales organizations, and dealerships. PICK operating system licensees include companies such as Microdata, Applied Digital Data Systems, Altos Computer Systems, General Automation, Ultimate Corporation, Pertec Computer Corporation, Computer Distributors, Inc., and Systems Management, Inc.

In the 1970s, the PICK operating system was normally sold under a name supplied by the licensee, such as "REALITY" (Microdata Corporation) and "Ultimate" (Ultimate Corporation). Today, PICK operating system implementations are often identified as "PICK" systems, regardless of the bundled system name or hardware.

Among the many features of the PICK operating system are:

1) A virtual memory management scheme that utilizes the entire hard disk as though it were main memory. This scheme efficiently schedules and controls the actual contents of RAM through a page swapping technique that is based on the least-frequently-used page algorithm.

2) A unique file structure that supports variable-length files, items (records), attributes (fields), values (portions of fields) and subvalues (portions of values).

3) A dictionary-based data retrieval language.

4) A sophisticated data base management scheme that pro-
    vides automatic space allocation for dynamic files.

5) An English-like, ad hoc, data retrieval language.

6) A stored procedure language.

7) A multilevel security system.

8) A sophisticated print spooler capable of addressing up
    to twenty different printer devices and managing over
    six hundred print image reports.

9) Support for up to 128 terminals, many types of parallel
    and serial printers, and a wide variety of ASCII
    terminals.

Hardware Environment

The minimum PICK execution environment requires at least 32K bytes
of RAM, one asynchronous ASCII terminal, a timer for the generation of interrupts, a hard disk, and at least one backup device.

The maximum configurations are implementation dependent, ranging
from table top systems to the IBM 4300 mainframe.

The PICK operating system provides an efficient means of sharing
and reusing main memory. Most PICK configurations include from 64K
to 512K bytes of main memory and 10-200 megabytes of disk storage.
The actual physical maximum of the main memory address space is dependent on the system processor (1-64 megabytes).

Job/Task Control

Process scheduling is provided by memory-resident monitor software.
Each process is allocated a time slice (measured in milliseconds)
prior to deactivation. The monitor further assigns priorities to a
process, depending on whether the process is interactive (e.g., a

data entry process) or noninteractive (e.g, a sort or report generation process). Scheduling is transparent to the user, but may be
altered by the user depending on his/her particular needs.

The PICK monitor code determines the priority status of a port
or process by determining whether or not the terminal is interactive
or noninteractive. Process priority is dynamic and a process is automatically "bubbled up" the priority queue upon keyboard input.

Portability

For most PICK implementations, application software can be ported
by simply recompiling the PICK/BASIC programs that make up the
application. In a few cases, minor syntactic modifications are also
needed in order to transport the application software.

Operating system software is written in PICK assembler and is
implementation independent. The operational characteristics remain
the same on virtually all PICK implementations.

PICK SYSTEMS also compiles its assembler source into object code
for the target processor. This capability greatly reduces the amount of
code that must be written for a new implementation and allows PICK
programmers to focus primarily on machine-dependent software (such
as I/O drivers). Once the I/O drivers and the necessary supporting
structures and translators are in place, the object code can be
downloaded from the PICK host to the target system.

Memory Organization

The PICK operating system is implemented in two forms, firmware
and software. In most mainframe and minicomputer implementations, the system is implemented in firmware—at the microinstruction level in ROM.

In microprocessor-based machines, the functions of the micropro-
grammed firmware are emulated in software. Software implementations generally require 32K bytes of RAM for storage of the
memory-resident code and tables. In both types of implementations,
a process control table and a memory management table are present
in main memory.

The memory resident software includes the following:

1) The "monitor" code. This software controls process scheduling and provides an I/O request interface.

2) Out-of-line firmware emulation code. This code emulates the PICK functions that are normally implemented in microinstruction ROM. This code, occupying roughly 6000 bytes of storage, is only present on software implementations.

3) Memory and process management code. This code provides functions such as memory management and process scheduling. This software occupies approximately 6000 bytes of storage.

4) Implementation-dependent routines and I/O drivers. These routines are specific to a particular processor and typically require from two to three thousand bytes of storage.

I/O Devices

The PICK operating system normally interfaces to asynchronous ASCII terminals, hard disks and flexible diskettes (both 5¼- and 8-inch), half-inch magnetic tapes, quarter-inch streaming cartridge tapes, serial printers, and parallel printers.

Field-developed interfaces include optical character recognition (OCR) devices, automated teller machines (ATM), point of sale (POS) terminals, high-speed synchronous modems, and various multiplexers and concentrators.

I/O device drivers are dependent on the choice of system hardware and are not provided by PICK SYSTEMS. PICK SYSTEMS provides the ported virtual operating system code and some device driver design assistance.

Software Support

PICK assembler language is the heart of the PICK system. A translator—for generating object code for the target system processor from PICK assembler source programs—is developed for each PICK operating system implementation. This language allows a programmer to address every critical element in the system. Licensees do not normally provide the PICK assembler language to end users in order to prevent misuse.

The PICK/BASIC language is a superset of standard Dartmouth BASIC. PICK/BASIC is ideally suited to dynamic array management of variable-length items (records) and files. This language is included with all PICK implementations and is an integral part of the system. Virtually all applications are written in PICK/BASIC, ensuring a high degree of compatibility among PICK systems, regardless of manufacturer.

The PROC interpreter is analogous to the Job Control Language (JCL) interpreter on a mainframe, allowing procedure definitions to be executed. For example, through PROC a user can control system reporting, system backup, and batch processing. PROC provides a high-level language with the capability of interactive (terminal formatting, input, and validation) or noninteractive execution modes.

ACCESS, an English-like retrieval language, provides a means of extracting, manipulating, and formatting output from dictionary-based files through a free-form English sentence structure. Each ACCESS input sentence is immediately compiled and interpreted, totally transparent to the operator. ACCESS also provides the capabilities for performing special operations on data, such as the application of algebraic formulae or the conversion of text strings to alternate formats.

The editor provides a means of entering documents, source programs, and stored procedures. The editor may also be used to update any data item on the system. Normally, however, this update function is managed by programs written in PICK/BASIC.

RUNOFF serves as the system's text formatter and document processor. In conjunction with the editor, RUNOFF is used to prepare documentation, manuals, letters, and other text-oriented materials. RUN-OFF supports automatic headings and footings, page numbering, column alignment, centering, index preparation, and underline/boldface type. In addition, RUNOFF can merge data from other files into the text.

System Security

Security is provided at an account level. Each user account on the system may contain an encrypted password that will be requested by the system each time a user logs onto the account. File-level security is discussed in the **File Access and Protection** section.

Libraries

Several files containing procedures, programs, and data are provided with the PICK operating system. These files include:

1) PROCLIB - Procedure library.

2) SYSPROG-PL - Procedure/program library.

3) ERRMSG - The text of error messages.

4) ACC - Accounting (usage) history.

5) POINTER-FILE - Lists data storage file.

6) SYSPROG - Maintenance account.

7) SYSTEM - Account definition file.

8) NEWAC - Verb/command definition file.

Diagnostics

The diagnostics process for PICK operating system software is a set of programs called Automated Test Procedures (ATP). This package exercises each function of the operating system and is typically used by PICK SYSTEMS as the acceptance criteria for a correct implementation.

System Generation

The PICK system is typically transported to a computer by means of a sysgen tape or diskette. This tape/diskette contains the following items:

1) Bootstrap section. This section provides enough information to start the monitor software and read the code that will load the rest of the media. This portion of generation also includes the function of "sensing" all attached hardware—including disks, I/O ports, and main memory—to establish the necessary tables and "workspace" areas needed for operation.

2) ABS section. ABS is an abbreviation for the absolute address of the virtual code that normally resides in the first 400 logical frames of the hard disk. Each frame of the operating system is loaded into its corresponding ABS address during the initial start-up procedure. Normally, the ABS section does not have to be reloaded during system operation.

3) FILE-SAVE section. This section contains the supporting accounts and files needed for operation. This section is structured in the same manner as the user's backup media. The system generation procedure pauses between each of the loading phases, prompting the operator to mount the appropriate tape or diskette. (During system generation, a user may replace the standard PICK FILE-SAVE tape with his/her own backup media in order to generate a customized system.) The process of reloading the data area from a FILE-SAVE tape or diskette is referred to as a "full restore." Users are advised to perform a full restore occasionally, as this procedure reorganizes the disk files and applies any "reallocation parameters" that may have been designated prior to the creation of the FILE-SAVE tape.

User Interface

All operations begin at a level referred to as the Terminal Control Language (TCL) level. This level is indicated to the user by means of the ">" prompt character.

Each user-entered instruction or command sequence is parsed by the TCL processor to separate and interpret the various parameters. Depending on the class of the command, several subsequent processes are activated.

Each "verb" (command) is stored in a file called the master dictionary (MD). The verb definition indicates the absolute address of the virtual code that supports the requested function. When a user enters a command, the command verb definition is found in the MD. (MD entries are hashed to improve speed.) Control is then transferred to the code specified in the verb definition. Some commands require an item name specification—in the form of an item identifier or a list of item identifiers. (An item identifier is the PICK equivalent of a key.)

PICK commands can be extremely simple. For example, the TIME command requires only one parameter:

>TIME <CR>
11:00:00 07 DEC 1983

More complex commands can be specified to ACCESS, the dictionary-driven, English-like data retrieval language processor. The generalized sentence structure for ACCESS allows the specification of the following:

1) A verb. An action-oriented command defining which ACCESS process to activate. Verbs include LIST, SORT, LIST-LABEL, SORT-LABEL, T-DUMP, COUNT, etc.

2) A filename. The name of the file from which the data is to be retrieved.

3) Selection criteria. A set of parameters to limit the set of data to be retrieved.

4) Sequence criteria. For sorting commands, the sequence criteria specify the sort key or keys for producing the data in a specific sequence.

5) Output fields. The name or names of the data fields (called "attributes") to output. These names are defined by the user and stored in the dictionary level of the previously-specified filename. These items define both the location of a data item and any special functions to perform on the data prior to output.

6) Modifiers. Modifiers allow a user to specify special reporting functions, such as the definition of report headings and/or footings, columnar totals, and output device routing.

7) Options. Options allow the user to specify functional operations (e.g., directing the output to the terminal or printer). Most of the options have an "English-like" equivalent in the form of a modifier. Modifier vs. option use is left to the user's personal preference.

For example, the following is a valid ACCESS command containing a verb, filename, selection criteria, sequence criteria, report output attributes, and modifiers:

```
>SORT CUSTOMER-FILE WITH INVOICE.AMOUNT > "0" AND WITH
RECEIPT.AMOUNT = "0" BY CUSTOMER.NAME BREAK-ON CUSTOMER.NAME
INVOICE.DATE TOTAL INVOICE.AMOUNT TOTAL RECEIPT.AMOUNT CONTACT.NAME
PHONE.# HEADING "PAGE 'P' CUSTOMERS WITH INVOICES DUE PRINTED AT
'DL'" LPTR
```

The Virtual System Debugger

The system debugger is capable of addressing and updating/displaying any element of data on disk or in memory. Data elements can be specified symbolically or directly, by address.

The debugger also supports breakpoints, traces, iteration control, and direct program instruction address branching.

The PICK/BASIC Symbolic Debugger

The PICK/BASIC debugger allows a user to debug application software written in PICK/BASIC source code. Through this debugger, every program variable is accessible to the programmer for interrogation and/or modification.

The PICK/BASIC debugger supports breakpoints, traces, interactive and symbolic debugging, iteration control, display of program source text, and direct program instruction address branching.

Data Structures

The PICK operating system organizes data into logical pages (or "frames"), typically in increments of 512 bytes per page. Each of these 512-byte pages stores 500 bytes of data, including the special system delimiters used to define the beginning and the end of items and attributes. The first 12 bytes of each data frame are reserved as a linkage field. The linkage field contains "forward" and/or "backward" linkage pointers to other frames when data crosses a frame boundary.

Data (record) storage supports variable length files, items (records), attributes (fields), values (portions of an attribute), and subvalues (portions of a value).

The File System

Files are defined by pointers to absolute locations on the physical disk drive and stored as descriptive item identifiers in a user's master dictionary. There are two types of file pointers. The first, and most frequently used, is referred to as a "D" pointer. A "D" pointer indicates that the file was created from the current account name. The second type of file pointer is a "Q" pointer. This file pointer allows an account to access a file that was created on a different account. This file pointer differentiation is transparent to the user. The difference is only important to the backup processor, which saves all of the "real" (D-type) files for a particular account.

Every item written to, or retrieved from, disk goes through the PICK "hashing algorithm." Using this algorithm, each item identifier (key) is "hashed" into a group (a portion of a file) and then added as the last item in the group.

As an item is written to disk, the system calculates the size of the item (in bytes) and appends a 4-byte "byte count" field to the beginning of the item. This byte count field defines not only the item's size, but exactly where the beginning of the next item in the group will be found.

The variable-length, three-dimensional record structure is implemented by using a special set of characters as reserved system delimiters. These characters define the separation of attributes (fields), values, and subvalues. By using a delimiter to define the end of a field, the system does not have to store any more data (i.e., pad characters) than is actually defined in the field.

Scheduling Techniques

Each process is allocated a "time slice" whenever the process is activated. Normally, the time slice for an interactive process is several times greater than the time slice for a batch process. This difference prevents batch processes from degrading system throughput.

An interactive process is deactivated when any of the following conditions exist:

1) A disk request is issued. The process is reactivated as soon as the requested frame is found.

2) The time slice is exhausted.

3) The user voluntarily terminates a time slice.

Memory and Resource Management

The PICK operating system automatically keeps track of unused system disk space in the "overflow" table. This table contains the disk locations at which contiguous and/or linked frames of available space are located. In allocating space, the system depletes whichever overflow block is closest to the requirements of the requesting process.

The PICK operating system uses a virtual memory management scheme. In this scheme, the disk is divided into 512-byte pages that can be "paged in" to a main memory buffer.

Each 512-byte page allows the storage of 500 bytes of data, including system-supplied delimiters. The first 12 bytes of a frame are reserved for "linkage" fields. When a record does not physically reside in a frame, the system automatically "attaches" a frame (called a "linked" frame) and updates the "forward" link in the first frame, and a "backward" link in the (overflow) frame. This process is repeated as necessary. As such, there is no limit to the number of items that can be stored in a file.

When a process requests a record from a disk file, the system hashes the item identifier to the "group" in which the item (record) will be found. Having found the actual disk address of the group, the system accesses the Hash Address Table (HAT), to see if the frame is already in main memory. If the frame is already in memory, the data is made available to the requesting process. If the frame is not in memory, it must be brought into memory from the disk. (If main memory is physically full, the system automatically "flushes" the least-frequently accessed frame that is currently resident in main memory.)

In the event that the data item is not main memory resident, and the item was not found in the first frame of the group, the system begins a lateral, sequential search of each item identifier in the designated group, by paging in another data frame. If the specified record is found in the frame, the user's process is reactivated, allowing further processing on the data. If the record is not found, the "forward link" field is checked, and the frame specified in the linkage is paged into main memory, if it is not already present.

Garbage Collection

The only process that requires garbage collection is PICK/BASIC. Each variable in a program is assigned a storage location, normally requiring less than 50 bytes. As a string or variable increases in size, it is automatically moved to either a 150- or 250-byte storage area. If a string or variable increases in size beyond 250 bytes, it is automatically moved to a "free storage" area where it can continue to grow—to a maximum of 32,000 bytes.

Resource Management

The operating system supports device-independent software by allowing a user to direct the output from a process to a device by simply naming the device prior to execution of the process.

The File System

The PICK operating system has four file levels:

SYSTEM

MD (Master Dictionary)

Dictionary

Data

Each level of this file structure defines the next lower level and has certain features and functions:

1) SYSTEM. This file level defines the disk locations of each individual "account" on the system—along with the associated access and retrieval codes, the password, the privilege level and the accounting history update options.

2) Master Dictionary. This file level defines all files associated with an account—verb definitions, pointers to any files "outside" of the account, and pointers to procedures that function like verbs.

3) Dictionary. This file level defines the location of the individual fields within a data file, along with a pointer to where the data file is located.

4) Data. This file level is where data actually resides, stored in the PICK file structure format.

File Definition

Files are defined under the TCL processor by means of the CREATE-FILE command. In the creation of a file, several parameters must be specified. These parameters include:

1) Filename. Any combination of alphanumeric characters, with a maximum length of 50 characters.

2) Modulo. The number of contiguous groups (frames) to allocate to the file. The current maximum modulo is 32K. This parameter may be changed at any time for a more efficient "distribution" of items in a file.

3) Separation. The number of frames per group, normally one.

Note that the modulo and separation parameters are specified individually for both the dictionary and the data levels of a new file.

File Access and Protection

All PICK files support random access operations. Files are maintained from TCL with the following commands:

>CREATE-FILE
>DELETE-FILE
>CLEAR-FILE

TCL commands that access files automatically open and close files as needed during processing.

The PICK operating system provides an access/update protective mechanism for data files. This scheme defines whether a user may "access only" or "access and update" a file from a particular account.

References

The IDBMA Directory of PICK/Reality Hardware Systems and Services, International Data Base Management Association, 1983.

The IDBMA Directory of PICK/Reality Software, International Data Base Management Association, 1983.

Operating Software by PICK SYSTEMS: An Overview of the PICK Operating System, PICK Systems, 1983.

The Second Decade: Move Over Herman, PICK Systems, 1983.

Sisk, J., The PICK Pocket Guide, PICK Systems, 1982.

Sisk, J., The Reality Pocket Guide, JES & Associates, Inc., 1982.

Truax, P., "Generic Operating Systems: Bringing the Pieces Together in Office Systems," Computerworld, November 29, 1982.

Jonathan Sisk began working with the PICK Operating System in 1979, in the area of applications programming. He joined the technical support staff of Microdata Corporation in late 1979 and provided technical support and presentations to end users, dealers, and direct sales outlets. In 1981, Jonathan formed JES & Associates, Inc., specializing in services and software for the PICK Operating System. Since then, Jonathan has written the PICK Pocket Guide and the REALITY Pocket Guide, and now provides technical training seminars to end users and many of the PICK Licensees.

William W. Walsh serves as marketing vice president and is also responsible for planning and product implementation. He has been involved with the PICK Operating System since 1971 when, at Microdata, he was instrumental in the development of the PICK-based REALITY system. He holds a B.S. degree in Electrical Engineering from the University of Notre Dame, an M.B.A. in Finance from Saint Louis University, and an M.S. degree in Management Science from United States International University.

Kenneth O. All is director of corporate communications at PICK SYSTEMS. He gained his first experience with the PICK operating system while serving as an agency public relations account manager for Microdata in 1976. Prior to joining PICK in 1982, Kenneth held management and creative positions in advertising and public relations with firms such as Control Data, International Rectifier, and General Dynamics.

Chapter 6

THE polyFORTH OPERATING SYSTEM

*A High-performance Multiuser System
for Real-time Applications*

Elizabeth D. Rather
FORTH, Inc.

6

The polyFORTH system is a complete, integrated programming environment that includes a multiprogrammed operating system, a FORTH high-level language compiler, a resident assembler, and many utilities. polyFORTH combines the concept of a fully-integrated programming environment with the high performance required for demanding real-time applications.

polyFORTH is available in two versions. polyFORTH II executes on most 8- and 16-bit processors; polyFORTH/32, available for the Motorola 68000 and the NCR 9300, is an enhanced version that features 32-bit addressing and 32-bit-wide stacks. These systems, introduced in 1982, represent the fourth generation of systems offered by FORTH, Inc. since the company was founded in 1973 by the original developers of the FORTH language.

Some key features of polyFORTH are:

1) Hardware requirements. Development systems require only 32K bytes of memory, with nearly 16K available for user programs. Disk drives are required for program support, but not for PROM-based applications. The run-time nucleus may be as small as 1K bytes.

2) Multiprogramming support. Any number of asynchronous tasks can run concurrently. These tasks may support multiple users on even the smallest hardware configurations.

3) Real-time performance. Real-time performance is achieved by a fast event-driven scheduling algorithm, zero-overhead interrupt processing, and the use of assembly language code for all time-critical operations.

4) Market applications. polyFORTH is designed to be used in all real-time applications, including process control, robotics, data acquisition/analysis, scientific/medical instrumentation, and communications.

5) PROMable code. polyFORTH Level 4 systems may run in PROM. Target applications may include any subset of polyFORTH features, such as the disk handler, the serial I/O device drivers, the interactive human interface, over 400 primitive operations, and even (under special license) the FORTH compiler and assembler—to provide end user programmability.

6) Compatibility. polyFORTH contains all the principal features of the FORTH-83 international standard. polyFORTH II systems are mutually compatible on all processors; polyFORTH/32 systems are also mutually compatible. Moreover, polyFORTH/32 systems can execute polyFORTH II applications with minor modifications.

7) Size. The minimum polyFORTH II target nucleus requires only 1K bytes while the minimum polyFORTH/32 nucleus needs 1.5K bytes. The full nucleus requires 8K bytes and 16K bytes for polyFORTH II and polyFORTH/32, respectively. A complete polyFORTH II system typically uses 10K-12K bytes of memory while a polyFORTH/32 system uses approximately 32K bytes. Finally, polyFORTH II requires at least 32 bytes of RAM per task; poly-FORTH/32 requires 48 bytes.

polyFORTH is a multiuser, multitasking operating system. Programming is supported by a FORTH high-level language compiler, a FORTH assembler, and a bi-level interpreter. The system also includes a string-oriented editor, a disk copy utility, and a program listing utility. Over 400 resident commands are supplied as standard equipment, along with a math library and a data base support system.

In addition to more than 1000 pages of printed documentation, the system supports on-line interactive documentation. Sixty days of free hot-line support are included when the system is purchased. A polyFORTH user can optionally obtain a one year support contract (with system upgrades), introductory FORTH courses, advanced FORTH courses, and consulting/programming services.

Memory Organization

Figure 6-1 contains a diagram of the memory organization for a typical multiuser polyFORTH system. The actual sizes of the various components are user-configurable to suit the demands of a particular application.

The nucleus of a FORTH system requires 8K bytes on 8- and 16-bit processors and 16K bytes on 32-bit processors. The nucleus—the only portion of the system that is normally stored in binary form— is either PROM-resident or booted from disk. The nucleus contains the FORTH compiler, the text interpreter, the address interpreter, several hundred elementary operators (for common functions such as arithmetic), disk and terminal drivers, the multiprogrammer, the text editor, and (on most systems) the assembler. These routines are

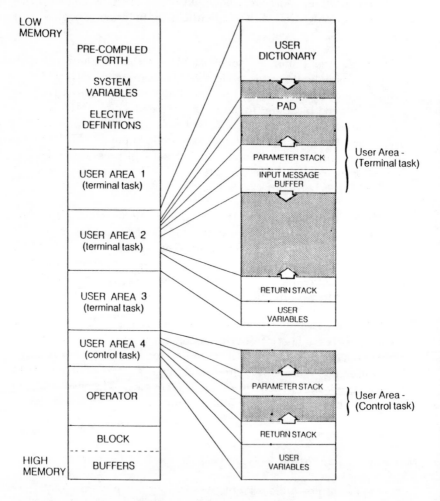

Figure 6-1 The Memory Organization of a Typical Multiuser polyFORTH System.

all reentrant and are globally available. The source code for the nucleus is written in FORTH and its assembly language. (This source is available at extra cost.)

Following power-up or a bootstrap load, a set of commonly-used routines is loaded. These "elective" routines contain such functions as extended precision arithmetic, clock and calendar support, the definitions of the specific multiprogrammed tasks in use, and application routines that are available to all system users. Routines in this section are fully reentrant and globally available. Source for these elective routines is included on all polyFORTH systems.

A small region of RAM contains a global set of vectors that control central system functions, such as disk I/O. In high memory, there are four 1024-byte buffers used for disk I/O. (The number of buffers may be adjusted by the user.)

User Dictionary, Scratch Pad, Stacks, and Variables

Each user in the system has a private dictionary of routines, which is linked to the dictionary of globally available nucleus routines and elective routines. In a software development environment, this dictionary would contain the routines that are under development by a programmer; in a multiuser application, these routines might be a subset of the application software (organized as an overlay). Routines in a user dictionary are not normally accessible to other users in the system.

Each user also has a local "scratch pad" region (named PAD) that is used by most string handling operations. The string editor uses this region to hold several buffers during operation.

All tasks have a pair of push-down stacks that control task functions. The "parameter stack" is the main set of working registers—used to pass parameters between FORTH routines. The "return stack" controls the logical program flow through FORTH routines, loops, etc.

Each task also has a region of variables used by routines in the reentrant shared dictionary. Some of these variables control hardware operation (e.g., special VDT functions), while other variables control software or system functions (e.g., number conversions or file accesses). About one-fourth of this variable region is available for application-specific user variables.

Disk I/O

One of FORTH's key features is its simple and efficient standard virtual memory format that maximizes transportability across many different types of mass storage devices. Central to this standard is the organization of mass storage media into 1024-byte **blocks**. Blocks normally reside on disk devices. The system provides two or more memory-based disk buffers; blocks are automatically read into these buffers when the blocks are referenced. Each block has a fixed block number, which is a direct function of the block's physical location on the mass storage media. If a block is modified in a memory buffer, the block will automatically be replaced on disk before the buffer is reused. In this manner, explicit reads and writes are not required; the programmer may presume that data is in memory when referenced. The common block size helps make applications easily transportable.

A block is analogous to a standard sector in a CP/M file. Since the block number maps directly to the physical location, however, block access doesn't require a directory or chaining logic. The poly-FORTH system disk drivers also optimize sector mapping to provide high-speed sequential block accesses. As a result, polyFORTH offers better disk performance than many conventional operating systems.

The 1K-byte block size is a convenient unit. For example, FORTH source code is stored in blocks and the standard editor formats this text into 16 lines of 64 characters each for display and editing. Blocks usually contain several related routines, forming a syntactic unit that roughly corresponds to a paragraph of prose. Groups of blocks are "loaded" together to comprise an application. This loading process simply directs the text interpreter to process the specified application text and compile the results into memory in a directly executable form.

Blocks are also used to store data. A programmer can combine small records into a block or spread large records over several blocks. The data base support system (described in a later section) provides a convenient vocabulary for defining and accessing such records.

Serial I/O

The standard serial I/O protocol in polyFORTH allows applications to communicate with printers, printing terminals, "intelligent" ter-

minals, "dumb" terminals, modems, etc. This protocol assumes minimal intelligence in the external device. The protocol also provides
a list of vectored routines so that the task supporting each serial
port may have its own private set of hardware-specific functions
(transparent to the software). The serial I/O functions include:

Command	Description
c EMIT	Transmits an ASCII character ("c") to the task's serial port.
a n TYPE	Transmits a string (of length "n" at address "a") to the task's port.
KEY	Awaits one keystroke from the task's keyboard and returns the received ASCII code on the stack.
a n EXPECT	Awaits a string (of length "n") from the keyboard and places the received characters in memory (at address "a").
CR	Performs a "new-line" function (carriage return and line feed, or equivalent).
PAGE	Performs a "new-page" function (clear screen, form feed, or equivalent).
r c TAB	Positions the cursor to row "r", column "c."

Actual processing of incoming and outgoing characters is normally
interrupt-driven. In this manner, when a task is inactive waiting
for an I/O interrupt, other tasks can execute.

Multitasking and Multiprogramming

polyFORTH is designed to support any number of concurrently-
executing asynchronous processes. The entity executing a process is
called a task. Each task has its own stacks and user variables. Depending on the task's particular needs, the stacks and user variables

may be defined to have different sizes; the minimum total task size is approximately 32 bytes. The number of tasks that may be defined is limited only by the available hardware resources (e.g., memory).

There are two types of tasks: terminal tasks and background tasks. Terminal tasks can support a serial I/O port, and hence a human user. These tasks require a larger user area than background tasks require. Terminal tasks can also have a private dictionary of commands. Background (or "control") tasks, on the other hand, do not have access to a serial I/O port. Background tasks have smaller and simpler user areas. Background tasks are normally used to control hardware functions.

Tasks are linked in a round-robin fashion. Normally, all tasks operate with the same priority. Access to the processor is granted on an event-driven basis. A task that is running will continue to run until it requests an I/O operation, requests a specified time delay, or executes the word PAUSE, which temporarily relinquishes the processor. If a task is awaiting I/O, the interrupt that signals I/O completion will mark the task "ready" and the task will be activated on its next round-robin turn.

This algorithm was designed to maximize service to all tasks. The round-robin polling cycle requires only one machine instruction per task. Similarly, the process of activating and deactivating tasks is extremely simple; Table 6-1 lists the number of instructions required for some typical microprocessors.

| Microprocessor | Number of Machine Instructions | |
	Activate	Deactivate
8080/Z80	17	16
8086/88	9	5
LSI-11	7	4
6800	19	12
6809	9	4
68000	9	5
1802	15	10

Table 6-1   The Number of Instructions Needed to Activate and Deactivate polyFORTH Tasks for Some Common Microprocessors.

Since all tasks share the same routines in the reentrant dictionary, all tasks have equal access to application variables that influence their actions. No special structures are needed for inter-task communication. The principal commands for task control are:

Command	Description
t ACTIVATE	Starts the task (named "t").
PAUSE	Deactivates the current task for one pass through the round-robin queue and allows other tasks to run. This command is used in processor-intensive routines to optimize overall performance.
n MS	Deactivates the current task for a specified number of milliseconds.
STOP	Deactivates the current task indefinitely (i.e., until an interrupt or ACTIVATE awakens the task).

Interrupts

The polyFORTH system includes a standardized method for servicing hardware interrupts. There is no software interposed between the occurrence of the interrupt and execution of the interrupt service code except when the hardware supports only a single interrupt and the interrupting device must be identified by polling. In this case, a standard polling routine is executed to transfer control to the device-specific code.

Device drivers assume that tasks, executing high-level FORTH routines, are responsible for device control and that these tasks will request device action. A device request is normally made by a code routine that terminates with a call to the "deactivating" code in the multiprogrammer. The task will remain inactive until the device has signaled completion by means of an interrupt. The interrupt code performs any necessary immediate action and "wakes" the inactive task (see Figure 6-2). The awakened task will continue executing its routine and complete any additional processing that is required. Typical interrupt latency (from the interrupt until the task resumes execution) is less than a millisecond.

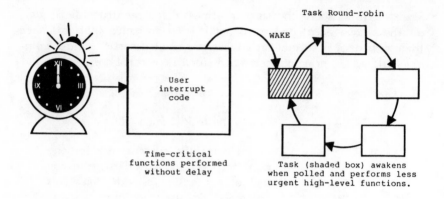

Figure 6-2 Example of a Timer Interrupt Waking a Task.

Some devices (such as disk drives) must be shared by several tasks. A simple protocol is used to resolve potential conflicts between these tasks. This protocol preserves the identity of the task currently using the device so that the interrupt code will always wake the correct task.

Target Compiling

polyFORTH supports two methods for preparing a binary object program for future execution. Both methods assume that the entire program is to be saved—compilation in FORTH is fast enough that the effort required to maintain libraries of precompiled routines on disk is not justified.

The turnkey compiler, shown in Figure 6-3, saves (on disk) a binary image of the program (polyFORTH plus the application) that is currently compiled and executing. The saved program may subsequently be booted and run. The program's image necessarily includes all of the polyFORTH operating system. The program is not ROMable because the variables and defined commands are intermingled.

The target compiler, on the other hand, compiles the object program entirely from source, starting with those FORTH primitives that will be required for the program's execution. (See Figure 6-4.) FORTH routines required for development support need not be included in the resulting object code—complete applications may run in under IK bytes. The object code is ROMable and may run in a hardware environment that is quite different from the host system.

The target compiler includes the complete source for the polyFORTH system. Thus, a developer may use the target compiler to recompile polyFORTH with modifications such as a different disk driver or a modified multiprogramming algorithm. For example, the target compiler is commonly used to modify polyFORTH to execute on custom hardware.

The User Interface

A polyFORTH user may interact with the system in one of two ways: indirectly through an application written in FORTH and running in

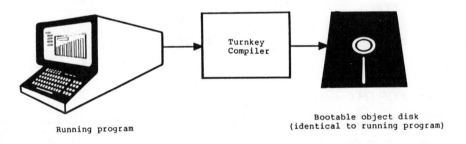

Figure 6-3   The Turnkey Compiler Saves a Bootable Image of an Executing Program.

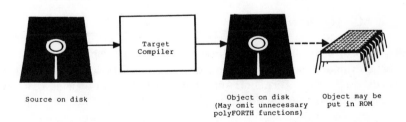

Figure 6-4   The Target Compiler Translates FORTH Source into ROMable Object Code.

the polyFORTH environment or directly by means of FORTH commands. The first method is entirely under the control of the programmer and may involve any combination of function keys, menus,
or—the preferred method—a special vocabulary of English commands specific to the application.

The programmer communicates with polyFORTH by using commands
or "words" found in a dictionary. These words are, in fact, elements
of the FORTH language. As shipped, polyFORTH systems include
about 500 such words. Typically, a programmer will add many more
words in the course of developing an application. The finished application will be fully controlled by a relatively few commands at the
top of a pyramid of defined words. During development, all words are
accessible at all times. The developer, however, can restrict the end
user to a small dictionary subset.

In FORTH, a word is any string of characters bounded by spaces.
Any character can be included in a word or can begin a word; there
are no "special characters" whose use is restricted. Thus, characters
that represent arithmetic operators or resemble punctuation can be
words if bounded by spaces. For example, the following line contains
seven FORTH words:

    FORTH begin + ? 3.14 (CR) EMPTY-BUFFERS

The FORTH Language

The polyFORTH operating system and the FORTH language are in-
timately connected. The system, the compiler, and the application
commands are indistinguishable and follow the same simple, consistent syntax. The following paragraphs provide a brief overview of the
FORTH language.

The FORTH Dictionary

The FORTH dictionary is a threaded list of variable-length items.
The dictionary is extensible and grows toward high memory as new
words are added. Terminals may have private dictionaries as mentioned in a previous section.

Special "defining words" are used to add new words to the dictionary.
The most common defining word is ":" (colon). The execution of ":"

causes FORTH to construct a dictionary entry for the word following the colon, as shown in Figure 6-5. The definition of this new word, in the form of pointers to previously-defined words, is also placed in the dictionary. A definition is terminated by ";" (semicolon). Words such as "ABC" in Figure 6-5 act as verbs, causing FORTH actions. (Definitions can also name variables or constants.)

One of FORTH's most powerful and unusual features is the language's extensibility. Users can not only extend the language by adding new commands, but they can also define new types of commands. This capability is similar to the data type definition facility in the Pascal and Ada languages. And, unlike most other languages, new FORTH definitions are not constrained in any way. For example, a user can define a special type of automatically indexed array. Or, a word that "names" the bits of an I/O interface port can be defined so that whenever the name is used, the correct bit values are read and returned.

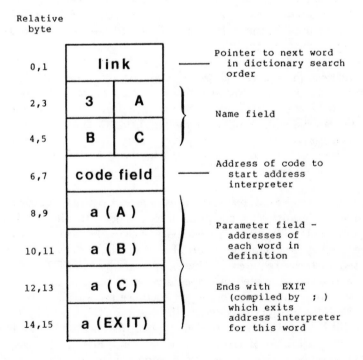

Figure 6-5 An Example of a FORTH Dictionary Entry.

FORTH Interpreters

FORTH is primarily an interpretive language—program execution is controlled by data items rather than by machine code. Although many interpreters are slow, FORTH avoids interpreter speed bottlenecks by maintaining two levels of interpretation.

The first level is the text interpreter. The text interpreter operates in a conventional manner, parsing text strings from terminals or mass storage devices and looking up each word in the dictionary. When a word is found, its definition is executed (unless the task is operating in the compile mode as discussed below) by invoking the address interpreter.

The address interpreter interprets strings of addresses by executing the definition pointed to by each address. Most dictionary definitions contain addresses of previously-defined words, which are, in turn, executed by the address interpreter. This mode of execution requires no additional dictionary searches, since the previously-defined words have already been compiled. (The dictionary entry for each previously-defined word already contains addresses. When the word was defined, the text interpreter searched the dictionary for each word used in the definition and placed the resulting addresses in the dictionary entry.)

The address interpreter has several important properties. First, the address interpreter is fast. On many processors, the interpreter executes only one or two overhead machine instructions per word (in addition to the code implied by the word itself). On some processors, the address interpreter is slightly faster than a subroutine call —and because of the pushdown stack, there is no additional calling sequence overhead.

Second, the address interpreter uses compact definitions. Each word used in a definition is compiled into a single 16-bit cell (32 bits in polyFORTH/32). This size compares favorably with the code size generated by an assembler macro. For example, a 20 byte macro that is used 10 times requires 200 bytes of memory. In FORTH, this routine would be assembled into the same 20 bytes plus a 10-byte dictionary entry. In FORTH, however, each use requires only two bytes. So, the total memory needed for 10 uses in FORTH is 50 bytes (20 + 10 + 10*2)—a 4:1 memory savings. In addition, because FORTH supports the definition of large vocabularies in a natural and easy way, FORTH can be easier to use than a large library containing hundreds of small assembly language subroutines.

Finally, FORTH high-level definitions are machine-independent, since the definition of one word in terms of other previously-defined words does not depend on the processor that interprets the definition. As a result, most words in a FORTH application are defined by ":" and interpreted by the address interpreter. In fact, the address interpreter itself is defined in this manner.

Structured Programming

FORTH is a highly-modular, totally structured language that strictly adheres to the following principles:

1) All words must be defined before the words are subsequently referenced. This rule holds for operations, constants, variables, etc.

2) FORTH programming techniques encourage top-down design and bottom-up coding/testing to ensure maximum reliability.

3) Logical program flow is restricted to sequential, conditional, and iterative patterns. Predefined words are provided to implement the most useful program control structures.

4) FORTH encourages the programmer to work with many small, independent modules for maximum testability and reliability.

A FORTH Programming Example

The following FORTH definition is extracted from an actual telescope control application:

```
: TRACKING   TRACKER ACTIVATE   REFRESH BEGIN
    HA WANTED   DC WANTED
    CHANGED @ IF  0 CHANGED !  REFRESH  THEN
    SLOWLY  LOWER EXECUTE  10 0 DO  FAST LOOP  AGAIN ;
```

This text comprises the highest level definition that prescribes the behavior of the TRACKER task. This task is responsible for tracking

the telescope and maintaining a real-time VDT display showing the
status of both the telescope and its data system. The word TRACKING
is executed as part of the startup sequence for this system. This
word REFRESHes the display and enters an infinite loop that:

1) Computes new WANTED positions for each of the tel-
    escope's two coordinates of motion, hour-angle (HA) and
    declination (DC). These desired coordinates are used
    to update the telescope's actual position.

2) Checks the variable CHANGED for a nonzero value. This
    variable will be set by any other task that changes a
    major observing function. For example, CHANGED will
    be set if a new data acquisition mode is selected or if a
    new telescope position is requested. If CHANGED is
    nonzero, the screen is REFRESHed again to display the
    new information and CHANGED is reset. The FORTH
    words "@" and "!" fetch and store values, respectively.

3) Finally, the display is updated. SLOWLY changing items
    are updated and a vectored routine that displays data
    system information in the LOWER portion of the screen
    is EXECUTED. Next, the FAST changing items are dis-
    played ten times—resulting in a 10:1 ratio in display
    rates.

Most of the words in this example are part of the application vocabulary. Each word can be executed directly from a terminal during
testing. And, in fact, each component of these words can be similarly tested interactively—without any need for special testing
"harnesses" or separate debugging packages. Moreover, the application
can easily be changed. Yet, this simple task definition is one of the
longest and most complex definitions in the entire telescope control
application!

Data Base Support

Many data base management packages provide a predefined structure
of files and index methods into which the user must fit his/her data.
This approach often imposes some performance penalties when compared with a structure designed specifically to support the intrinsic
organization of the original data. The data base support system included with polyFORTH provides a set of tools that a programmer

can use to define an efficient, customized data base. First developed
in 1974, the data base system has been used on some extremely large
and complex data bases—such as one with 600 megabytes of data and
32 simultaneous users. The polyFORTH data base management system
provides the following features:

1) Named files. A file is a contiguous region of disk blocks
   whose size and location are controlled by the programmer.
   Contiguous files improve performance by minimizing disk
   head motion and eliminating unnecessary disk accesses for
   directory look-ups. A file becomes a "current file" when
   its name is invoked. No "open" or "close" procedures are
   necessary.

2) Records. Each file is organized into records of a fixed
   length. The effect of variable-length records may be
   achieved by chaining multiple short records. At any time,
   a "current record" is selected. Actual access to the
   data in a record is accomplished by referencing named
   record fields. Field accesses always reference the current record of the current file.

3) Record layout. A list of named record fields is compiled
   as a "record layout." Each field definition contains the
   field's offset from the beginning of the record. This template may be applied to any record for which the template
   is suitable. All record data is accessed by field name.
   Field names are independent of the actual relative location of the field within the record.

4) Field type. Several field types are available—8-, 16-, and
   32-bit binary integers and fixed-length strings.

5) Report generation. A report generator is included. The
   report generator provides automatic pagination, dating,
   line control, headings, columnar alignment, and sub-
   totaling.

6) File sharing. The data base is shared by all tasks on the
   system through reentrant accessing routines and common data buffers. Only one copy of a record may exist at
   one time. Sensitive processes such as index manipulation
   are protected by a lockout feature.

7) Error checking. The system checks for errors such as
   invalid or missing parameters, requests for records that

are not within the file, non-existent operators, missing keys, redundant entries, disk errors, etc. Application-dependent checks may also be added.

File Access Methods

FORTH provides the flexibility to define file structures and accessing techniques that are appropriate to the natural relations within the data base. The following techniques are commonly used with polyFORTH:

1) Direct access. All files may be treated as direct access files. Given a record number, the user may obtain access to that record "directly," without searches, directory references, or other intermediate steps.

2) Sequential access. All files may also be accessed sequentially—to take advantage of the natural record order. Since records are contiguous (there are no record links to process), this access method is fast.

3) Ordered index. An "ordered index" is maintained (sorted by key) for the file. Simpler than the ISAM access method, this access method provides a high-speed binary search capability. In addition, sequential reports can be obtained from ordered index files without sorting.

4) Hierarchical index. Multiple hierarchical indexes may be established for a file. Each hierarchical level may be direct or ordered (depending on the nature of the file data).

5) Hashing. Simple hashing algorithms may be used to provide very high-speed searches.

6) Chaining. Data records (e.g., all measurements for a given sample or all line items for an order) may be linked in any number of chains. Chains may be linked either in order of entry or by key—to provide ordered reporting without sorting.

References

Brodie, L., "FORTH Offers Unique Solutions to Many Software Programs," Computer Technology Review, Spring/Summer 1981.

Brodie, L., Starting FORTH, Prentice-Hall, New Jersey, 1981.

Dessey, R., and M. Starling, "Fourth Generation Languages for Laboratory Applications," American Laboratory, February 1980.

Harris, K., "The FORTH Philosophy," Dr. Dobbs Journal, September 1981.

Kogge, P.M., "An Architectural Trail to Threaded Code Systems," Computer, March 1982.

Moore, C.H., "The Evolution of FORTH - An Unusual Language," Byte, August 1980.

Pearlman, D., "FORTH Inspires a Fanatic Following," Personal Computing, September 1983.

Rather, E.D., "Controlling the Escalating Costs of Software Development," Defense Science 2001+, June 1983.

Ting, C.H., "Formal Definition of FORTH as a Programming Language," Dr. Dobbs Journal, February 1982.

Elizabeth D. Rather is president of FORTH, Inc. She has over twenty years experience in the computer industry. In 1970-1971 she assisted C. Moore with the initial development of the FORTH language at a government laboratory. In 1973, she was one of the co-founders of FORTH, Inc.

Chapter 7

THE p-System OPERATING SYSTEM

The Universal Operating System

Thomas Burger
SofTech Microsystems, Inc.

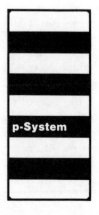

7

The p-System is a general-purpose, interactive, single-user, multi-tasking operating system that runs on many popular 8- and 16-bit microcomputers.

The object code portability provided by the p-System is so different from that achieved by other systems that the term "universality" is used to emphasize the distinction. System software and application programs generated by a p-System compiler can run without recompilation or modification on almost any microcomputer system that includes an 8080, a Z80, an 8086/8088, a 68000, a 6809, a 6502, or a 9900 processor. In addition, p-System software runs on HP87 and on LSI-11/PDP-11 computer systems.

The minimum configuration needed to support the p-System is 64K bytes of contiguous RAM, a console (keyboard and screen), and at least one disk drive. ROM-based versions of the system have been produced that eliminate the requirement for a disk drive, but, in general, at least one disk drive is required.

System Organization

The architecture of the p-System consists of three primary modules: the operating system, the p-machine emulator, and the Basic I/O System (BIOS).

The operating system and utilities are written in UCSD Pascal. The Pascal compiler translates these programs into machine code for a hypothetical processor called the p-machine. To install the operating system on an actual microprocessor, a p-machine emulator and a BIOS are written in the microprocessor's native code. The operating system and all its utilities are then ready to be run—without modification or recompilation. (The operating system and utilities can be transported without modification to any computer for which a p-machine emulator and a BIOS are available.)

As mentioned above, the p-machine emulator is written in the native code of the host CPU. The machine code for the p-machine (called **p-code**) is a binary code close to the native code of many common microprocessors; thus, p-code programs execute on the emulator faster than many source-code programs that run under an interpreter. The p-machine instruction set is compact, so p-code programs often use less memory than native code, particularly when the native code is produced by a high-level language compiler.

The p-machine emulator is independent of the I/O configuration of the particular system; thus, the p-machine emulator is transportable to any system that uses the same processor. For example, all 8086/8088-based machines use the same p-machine emulator.

The BIOS handles all low-level I/O services for the p-machine. The BIOS is written in the native code of the host computer and must be modified only when peripheral devices are changed.

Language Support

Compilers for UCSD Pascal, FORTRAN 77, BASIC, and LISP currently exist for the p-System. The UCSD Pascal, FORTRAN 77, and BASIC compilers form the "integrated languages." Each of these compilers supports separate compilation. This feature allows a program to be divided into separately compiled modules—each of which provides a set of services to the user—for easier development and maintenance. Programs can easily be constructed from these separately compiled modules (called **units**). The separate compilation feature allows users to modify or enlarge existing programs without recompiling all the units making up the program. p-System units provide the same benefits as Ada "packages" and Modula2 "modules." Moreover, the units from which a program is constructed may be written in any combination of Pascal, FORTRAN, or BASIC. In this way, each unit may be written in the language most appropriate for the task that the unit is to perform.

A unit is divided into two portions. One portion, the "interface section," declares the services provided by the unit. This information is needed by users of the unit. The other portion, the "implementation section," contains the internal implementation details of the unit. A user doesn't need to know these internal details in order to use the unit. In this manner, the implementation part of a unit can be modified without requiring recompilation of any programs that use the unit.

The p-code generated by the p-System compilers is very compact. For many processors, it occupies much less memory than either source code or machine code. The compute-bound portions of a program in p-code will execute more slowly than equivalent native code. But, overall performance may be better with p-code. For example, a large native code program may run more slowly than an equivalent p-code program if, because of its increased size, the native code program must frequently load overlays from the disk.

In many cases, only a small section of a program is critical to achieving performance objectives. What is needed is a means to use native code only in those critical sections and to use p-code for the remainder of the program. A set of utilities called native code generators are available for use in such situations.

A native code generator translates a p-code program into a mixture of p-code and native code. Once a p-code program has been translated into native code, universality has been sacrificed for performance efficiencies. The native code generators can be run on any processor, but the native code that they generate can run only on the target processor for which the code was generated.

In order to use the native code generators, native code generator information must be included with the program. This information is included by using compiler directives to indicate the portions of the program that are to be translated to native code. In many cases, the developer will include native code generator information with the program but will not perform the actual translation. This way, a single version of the program is distributed and the end user can apply the appropriate native code generator if he/she so desires.

Even though native code generator information may be included with a program, the program is still a machine independent p-code program until it is translated by a native code generator. The developer may selectively translate only parts of the program into native code—to optimize certain time-critical portions while retaining the more compact p-code for the remainder. Although native code may execute faster than p-code, it typically occupies 1.5 to 3 times as much memory.

Assemblers are available for each of the processors on which the p-System is supported. Like the native code generators, the assemblers can be run on any processor, but the code that an assembler generates will execute only on a single type of host processor. The assemblers can generate either relocatable or absolute object code. Relocatable code contains information that allows the system to place the code in any available area of memory; absolute code must be loaded into a specific area of memory.

A linkage-editor utility is used to link assembly language routines into high-level language units. Linking is only necessary for units or programs that use assembly language routines.

Units are compiled in such a way that it is unnecessary to link or bundle them together when forming a complete program. Units are called in as needed by means of a virtual reference scheme. Each unit contains a table indicating the names and virtual numbers of all the units it references. When a program is invoked, the operating system searches these unit-reference tables and locates the appropriate units. Tables, which map virtual numbers into physical unit locations, are then constructed in main memory. These tables allow calls and other inter-unit references to reach the correct destinations.

Each unit may directly reference up to 255 other units or segments, but there is no limit on the total number of units that can be employed in a given program. Since the units that make up a program do not have to be bundled together, sharing a single copy of a unit among several programs is a common and useful practice. All the units that make up a given program must be present when the program is invoked. But, all these units need not be located on the same I/O device as the program.

Another advantage of this virtual reference scheme can be seen when a commonly-used unit must be changed. Assuming that the change does not affect the interface portion of the unit, all programs that reference the changed unit will automatically use the new version as soon as the unit has been recompiled.

Command Format

The operating system and the system utilities are all menu driven. A prompt line is always presented at the top of the screen and all commands are invoked by single keystrokes. The organization of the commands is hierarchical; each command will either cause an action to occur or bring forth a new prompt line (at a lower level in the hierarchy). For example, the main system prompt presents the menu:

```
Command: E(dit, R(un, F(ile, C(omp, L(ink, X(ecute, A(ssem, D(ebug,? [IV.2 Rl.2]
```

Pressing "E" for Edit will invoke the system editor. The editor will, in turn, present the following prompt:

>Edit: A(djust C(opy D(el F(ind I(nsert J(ump K(ol M(argin P(age ? [7R0.5]

Prompt line control is one of the many standard screen handling services provided by the operating system and is available for use by any program.

Program Debugging

The symbolic debugger is a tool for debugging compiled programs and is invoked from the main system prompt line. The debugger allows a user to display and/or alter memory, set breakpoints, and single-step through a p-code program.

Memory locations are specified by entering either the name of a variable or an address. Breakpoints may be set by line number (as shown on a compiler listing) or by procedure number and code offset (from the beginning of the procedure). Whenever a breakpoint is encountered or an error occurs, the debugger is re-invoked.

Concurrency

Although the p-System is not a multiprogramming system, it does provide many services traditionally offered by multitasking or concurrent operating systems.

Concurrency provides a way to deal with external, asynchronous events. For example, the p-System's print spooler uses the system's concurrency facilities to allow the user to edit a text file while printing another file at the same time. The print spooler executes and "spools" text files to the printer while the system is waiting for the user to enter data from the keyboard.

Processes are declared much like procedures in UCSD Pascal and are set into action by the intrinsic START. A single process may be started many times should it be desirable to do so. The number of processes that may be active at any one time is constrained only by the amount of available memory. When a process is started, it is assigned a priority and a separate stack area. Both the priority and the size of the stack area are selectable by the programmer.

Semaphores are used to synchronize cooperating processes and to control critical sections of code. Semaphores may also be associated with an external event or an interrupt. Whenever this external event occurs, the associated semaphore is signaled. A process may synchronize with the event by waiting on that semaphore. This signaling facility allows a process to be used as an interrupt handler.

A task switch will only occur when a process waits on a semaphore or a semaphore is signaled. No time slicing is automatically performed. Whenever a signaled semaphore causes a process to be made ready to run, the system examines all processes that are ready to run and allows the highest priority process to resume execution.

Memory Management

Main memory is managed by the operating system as three logically distinct areas: the heap, the stack, and the code pool. The heap provides dynamically allocated memory blocks, while the stack follows the first-in-last-out rule for the order of allocation and deallocation. The code pool, like the heap, is dynamically allocated and is used to hold code segments.

The heap is used for dynamically allocated memory. A program may request memory blocks of any size and later return this memory to the system without regard to the order in which the memory was allocated.

As mentioned earlier, each process has its own stack. The stack is used for procedure **activation records.** An activation record contains the local data for the procedure, the procedure's parameters, and control information that is used to return to the calling procedure. In addition, the stack is used for expression evaluation. The stack always obeys the last-allocated-first-deallocated rule.

Dividing a program into units and segments overcomes the problems of a small main memory. This technique, however, raises the problem of managing memory in a way that meets the changing needs for data/instruction space. The p-System provides two solutions to this problem: internal and external code pools. Both solutions provide virtual memory management for p-System programs.

An internal code pool (see Figure 7-1) can expand, contract, or shift in response to program needs for stack and heap space.

The second solution provides an extended memory configuration (see Figure 7-2) in which the "external" code pool is entirely separate from the data area containing the stack and the heap. The architecture of this facility is such that a wide range of host processor memory organizations can be accommodated.

The dynamic and automatic management of code segments in the p-System is a significant aid to program developers. Very large programs can be built with much less concern for main memory constraints than is necessary in many other software environments. The same program can run in a 64K-byte Z80 environment and in a 128K-byte 68000 environment. The performance in each environment will differ, but the system will automatically adjust its memory management to exploit the memory resources of the host environment.

The p-machine architecture requires that a segment be located in main memory when it is executing. In addition, when a transfer of control between two segments takes place, both segments must be present during the transition. Much more space is usually available for the code pool than is necessary to meet these minimum constraints. In this case, as many of the most-recently used segments as possible are retained.

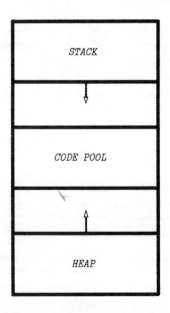

Figure 7-1 The p-System Internal Code Pool.

It is possible to override the operating system's least-recently used method for selecting which segment to remove from memory. This is accomplished by locking a group of one or more segments into memory. The list of segments that are locked in memory can be changed at any time and this list can include operating system segments in addition to application program segments. Only the segments that are not locked in memory are candidates for being swapped out of memory.

I/O Devices

All I/O devices are categorized as either communication volumes or storage volumes. The BIOS presents a uniform interface to all devices within each of these groups. For example, a printer and a terminal are both considered to be communication volumes and are accessed in exactly the same manner.

A communication volume is a character-oriented device such as a printer, terminal, or modem. For these devices, the BIOS interface provides the ability to read or write a sequence of characters.

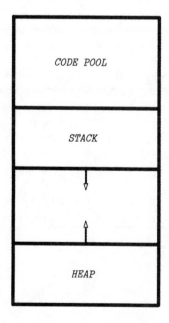

Figure 7-2 The p-System External Code Pool.

All storage volumes appear to the operating system as random access devices that are composed of 512-byte **blocks**. The actual device may be a hard disk, a diskette, RAM, or even tape. In the case of a diskette, the BIOS may perform logical sector interleaving and track-to-track skewing to improve performance. Storage volumes may have a capacity of up to 16 megabytes. The BIOS can support larger storage volumes by dividing a large physical volume into smaller logical volumes.

The p-System can support up to 127 logical devices. Each device has both a logical device number and a name. Communication volumes are assigned standard names while storage volumes have user-assigned names. The name of a storage device that contains removable volumes (such as a flexible diskette drive) is always the name of the currently mounted volume. A device's logical device number does not change.

Universal Medium

The many different disk formats currently in use hinder the movement of a portable program from one system to another. Some of the differences include the size of the diskette (8- and 5¼-inch), the number of sides, the recording density, the number of tracks, the number of sectors per track, and the size of each sector.

A special format for 5¼-inch diskettes, called the Universal Medium format, has been defined by SofTech Microsystems. This format can be supported by most 5¼-inch diskette drives/controllers. Many systems use the Universal Medium format as their native format; if not, a special utility program called an "adaptor" is used to move files between the Universal Medium format and the system's native diskette format.

By using the Universal Medium format, it is possible to distribute a single diskette that can be read by most systems that support 5¼-inch diskette drives.

I/O Redirection

Unless a program specifically designates a file for input or output, the system normally assumes that input is entered through the console keyboard and that output is directed to the console display. I/O redirection allows the source of the input and the destination of the output to be changed. Using this facility, the output of one program may be directed to the input of another program. (The user simply redirects output from the first program to a file and redirects input for the second program to the same file.) This facility is comparable to the "pipe" facility in the UNIX operating system.

Redirecting input amounts to driving the system with a "script." A script file is simply a text file containing input data that would normally be entered through the console. The Monitor command provides a convenient way for an operator to create a script file while using the system in a normal manner. Under the Monitor command, each operator keystroke is recorded in a script file. This recorded sequence of commands can then be repeated by redirecting input to the script file. The use of I/O redirection and script files offers many opportunities to increase operator productivity. As an example, automated regression tests for software maintenance use can save many hours of operator time.

File Systems

The file systems provide device independent I/O to both communication volumes and storage volumes. For example, a program can read a string of characters from a file without knowing whether the source of the file is the console keyboard or a disk file.

Storage volumes may contain many files. The p-System supports two ways of organizing the files on a storage volume—the standard file system and the advanced file system.

File names under both file systems may be up to 15 characters in length. A file name may include an optional suffix that indicates the type of the file. Any non-standard suffix is considered to indicate a data file. The standard suffixes are:

    .TEXT   Human readable text.

    .BACK   Human readable text (a backup copy).

    .CODE   Executable code (either p-code or machine code).

    .DATA   Data in a user-specified format.

Text files are organized into pages—each page is two blocks (1024 bytes) in length. The first page in the file is called the header page and contains information for use by the editors. The remaining pages in the file consist of a series of complete text lines, each of which is terminated by the carriage return character. Any unused space at the end of a page is filled with the NUL character. In order to save space when dealing with indented text, a blank compression code may be present at the beginning of a line. This blank compression code is the DLE character followed by a byte whose value is 32+n, where n is the number of characters to indent.

A code file is a file that contains either compiled or assembled code. Code files begin with a one-block header called a segment dictionary. This dictionary contains information used by the operating system and various utilities.

Data files may be structured in any way the creator of the file wishes. The operating system makes no assumptions about the content of a data file.

The Standard File System

The volume directory for a standard file system volume is a maximum of 2048 bytes in length. This directory contains both volume information and information about each file on the volume. The volume information consists of the volume name (up to 7 characters), the size of the volume in blocks, and the number of files in the directory. A directory may contain a maximum of 77 files. For each file, the directory contains the file name, the location of the file, the date the file was last modified, and the type of the file. All standard file system files occupy a contiguous group of blocks on the I/O device.

A duplicate directory may be maintained on a volume if the user desires. This duplicate directory is provided as a backup to aid in recovering accidentally deleted files. The duplicate directory is of the same format as the main directory. The utility COPYDUPDIR will replace the main directory with the duplicate directory. The utility MARKDUPDIR copies the current main directory into the duplicate directory. Thus, the user determines when the main directory is backed up and restored.

Two additional file name suffixes are recognized by the Standard File System:

.SVOL   A subsidiary volume file.

.BAD   A file covering a physically damaged area of a volume.

A subsidiary volume file is a file whose content has the same format as a volume. The purpose of subsidiary volumes is to provide two levels of directory hierarchy and to improve the system's ability to use large storage volumes. By using subsidiary volumes, the maximum number of files that can be contained on a volume is 5929. That is, the main volume directory may consist of 77 subsidiary volume files and each of these subsidiary volumes may contain 77 files.

Files that are marked as BAD files are used to cover physically damaged areas on a volume. A BAD file is considered to be unmovable. All other types of files may be moved in order to consolidate the free space on a volume.

The Advanced File System

In addition to the standard file system, an advanced file system is also available for the p-System. The advanced file system is ideal for large capacity storage volumes and removes many of the limitations of the standard file system. Since the capabilities of the advanced file system are a superset of the capabilities of the standard file system, programs that run under the standard file system will also run under the advanced file system with no modification or recompilation.

In the advanced file system, a tree-structured directory mechanism is employed that allows directories to be nested arbitrarily deep. A path name similar to the UNIX file naming convention is used to locate a file. Path names of up to 255 characters may be used.

The advanced file system is a B+/Tree-based file system and supports keyed file access as an integral part of the system. All files are represented as a B+ tree where the leaves of the tree contain record descriptors that point to the actual data. Directories are represented as keyed files in which the file name is the key and the data record

is the disk address of the root of the file. Since there is no arti-
ficial limit on the number of records in a keyed file, there is no limit
on the number of files that can be in a directory.

Keyed files may have variable length records and multiple records
with the same key. The basic operations that apply to keyed files
include sequential access in both ascending and descending key order,
random access, random record insertion, and a record update that
will expand the size of the record if needed.

A variety of directory information is maintained on each file. This
information includes the following:

1)   The date and time the file was created and last updated.

2)   A user-settable text comment that describes the file and
     is displayed in a directory listing.

3)   Other information that is used in performing consistency
     checks and that aids in recovering accidentally removed
     files.

Summary

The p-System is truly unique in that it provides object code portability to a variety of microcomputer systems—even when the systems
contain different microprocessors. With the application developer
freed from having to implement a new version of his/her software
package for each different system, the developer is able to devote
more attention to designing and implementing other applications.

The user-friendly, menu-oriented operator interface is an aid to both
experienced and novice users. A prompt line is always present as a
reminder of what commands may be entered, and only a single keystroke is needed to invoke a command.

The p-System provides sophisticated services that support both application execution and program development.

References

p-System Operating System Reference Manual, SofTech Microsystems.

p-System Program Development Reference Manual, SofTech
Microsystems.

p-System Internal Architecture Reference Manual, SofTech
Microsystems.

p-System Application Developers Manual, SofTech Microsystems.

Overgaard, M., and S. Stringfellow, Personal Computing with the
UCSD p-System, Prentice-Hall, Inc., New Jersey, 1983.

Thomas Burger is the supervisor of Product Enhancement at SofTech Microsystems, Inc. Prior to joining SofTech Microsystems, he was a systems programmer for Burroughs Corporation. Thomas has a M.S. degree in Computer Science from Vanderbilt University in Nashville, Tennessee and a B.S. degree in Mathematics from the University of Alabama in Birmingham.

Chapter 8

THE RM/COS OPERATING SYSTEM

*A Commercial Operating System for Multiuser,
Multitasking Business Computer Systems*

Thomas H. Morrison
Peter H. Ziebelman
Ryan-McFarland Corporation

RM/COS

8

The Ryan-McFarland Commercial Operating System (RM/COS) is a multiuser, multitasking operating system developed specifically for business computing requirements. (See Figure 8-1.) The RM/COS operating system is currently implemented on Texas Instruments' 990 and Business System computers and on Motorola M68000-based machines, including the Tandy Model 16, NCR Tower, Altos ACS68000, CIE 680 series, CYB Multibox, Wicat, and the IBM-PC (using the Sritek 68000 plug-in card).

The RM/COS operating system is designed for use with the RM/COBOL compiler and run-time support system. The RM/COS system provides the most efficient base for developing and executing software written in RM/COBOL. Applications may include any software written in RM/COBOL—ranging from vertical applications (such as accounts

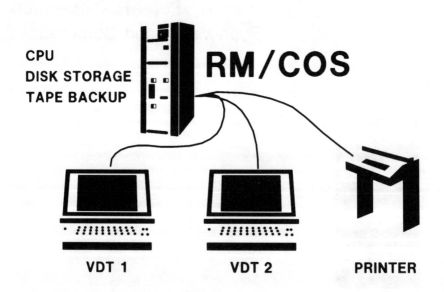

Figure 8-1 RM/COS is a Multiuser, Multitasking Operating System.

payable) to horizontal applications (such as code generators and spreadsheets). Since RM/COBOL is widely accepted as a highly portable COBOL compiler and run-time implementation, hundreds of applications are currently available.

The RM/COS operating system and utilities extend the concept of RM/ COBOL application code portability to the operating system. The applications developer and user can transport an entire software package —including job control language—quickly and efficiently. Software packages may be transported without rewriting either the job control language or the application itself. In addition, RM/COS permits media interchangeability among hardware systems—for example, the same 8" flexible diskette can be loaded into the Tandy system or into the Altos system.

Designed for the "desktop" computing environment, RM/COS satisfies multiuser and multitasking requirements with limited resident memory. For example, RM/COS can support two users in 64K-byte unmapped memory configurations and can provide a three-user diskette-based system in only 128K bytes of memory. Larger memory configurations can increase the speed and flexibility of the system. The RM/COS operating system is currently capable of supporting up to 99 terminals.

A typical RM/COS system implementation requires approximately 500K bytes of disk storage for the operating system and compiler. The complete resident memory requirements range from 32K bytes to 100K bytes, depending on the host system and the number and type of peripheral devices. A typical four-user system includes 256K bytes of resident memory, a 10M byte hard disk, and a flexible diskette or cartridge tape drive for program load and backup.

System Hardware Support

RM/COS supports the peripherals typically found in a business computing environment—terminals, printers, disk drives, and tape drives. RM/COS supports many popular terminals by providing the application program with a consistent "canonical" terminal representation. This canonical terminal consists of a standard display (24 rows by 80 columns) and a keyboard (with function keys). Each function is mapped into one or more keystrokes for a particular terminal type. For terminals without the entire repertoire of keys described by the canonical model, a "function sequence introducer" key is defined. Changing from one keyboard to another usually involves, at most, learning a new function sequence introducer. (See Figure 8-2.)

The canonical terminal is a benefit to both the end user and the application designer. The end user can "mix and match" VDTs as required, while the application developer need only write an application for one terminal—the canonical terminal.

The RM/COS system provides support for both parallel and serial printer interfaces. Disk devices include most 5¼- and 8-inch, single- and double-sided, single- and double-density diskettes and the popular hard disk technologies. RM/COS also supports cartridge tape drives. These drives may be used for backup/archival purposes or as file devices supporting multiple files per volume and multivolume files.

Data communications support is available for the popular 2780/3780 protocol through either the normal synchronous serial interface or an asynchronous serial interface. The asynchronous 3780 utility allows data interchange among computers without synchronous hardware. In addition, the asynchronous interface is available to COBOL application programs. Using this support, custom or proprietary protocols (such as those found in reservation systems or cash registers) can be implemented.

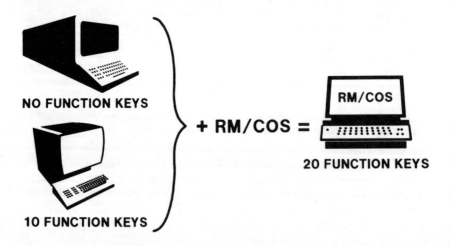

Figure 8-2   RM/COS Maps Existing Terminals into a Standard Canonical Representation.

Languages and Third-Party Software

The RM/COS operating system supports a superset of the GSA-certified RM/COBOL implementation as its high level language. RM/COBOL features:

1) A full "level 2" implementation of sequential, relative, and indexed files.

2) ANSI "level 2" SORT/MERGE capabilities.

3) Record- and file-level locking.

4) Standard CALL and CANCEL with no link-edit step.

5) Extended computational types including binary and packed decimal.

6) Full arithmetic capability including COMPUTE.

7) Library COPY.

8) Interactive debug and powerful interactive screen/keyboard handling.

Programmer access to additional system features for COBOL applications is available through COBOL-callable assembly language subroutines. Also, hundreds of third-party RM/COBOL commercial applications are available—ranging from agriculture software to wine cellar management software.

Two text editors are integral to the RM/COS operating system. The primary text editor is a full screen, character editor with many user-oriented features such as word wrap, word and columnar tabs, line markers, and floating left margin. In addition, the editor can copy, move, or delete a range of lines, insert from another file, duplicate or erase to a specified tab, find and replace strings (with a wild card matching capability), and split, join, and center lines. A profile feature allows the user to save frequently-used settings of the various screen editor features for recall in a subsequent edit session.

A line editor is provided for use with teletypewriter terminals—terminals that do not support cursor positioning. The line editor can also be used when editing must be performed in a batch mode (e.g., when an application vendor wishes to make minor modifications to customers' text files). The line editor has several features similar to those found in the full screen editor.

Print Spooling

The RM/COS system provides a print queue server subsystem to manage the system's printer resources. This subsystem consists of three main components: the queue entry mechanism, the queue server(s), and the queue manager. The queue itself is implemented as an ordinary indexed file. The queue entry mechanism is used to place a file print request in the queue. The entry mechanism also signals the other subsystem components when an entry has been added to the queue. The queue server selects qualified queue entries and prints the contents of the specified files using parameters extracted from the queue entries. Finally, the queue manager utility may be used to alter the entry selection criteria, add, modify, or delete queue entries, and communicate with the queue server(s) attached to the queue.

Other print server features include print-through (printing while the application is still generating the print file), single sheet feed, automatic page alignment, forms control, and specific device or device class selection. The entire subsystem is written in COBOL; source is supplied as an option, allowing an application designer to integrate the subsystem directly into a vertical product.

The print queue subsystem uses the generalized system features of shared files, record-level locking, and user events (described in later sections). These system features may also be used to write other queue serving subsystems—for example, a 3780 file transfer queue server.

The User Communication Link

A COBOL-callable subroutine provides direct application program control over the capabilities of an asynchronous, bit-serial communication port (user link). The programmer can specify speed and framing characteristics, can control link connection and disconnection, and can read or write data messages (terminated by user-specified codes). In addition, facilities are provided for both character and longitudinal data integrity checking. This subroutine allows a knowledgeable system designer to implement a custom bit-serial link interface.

System Generation

RM/COS does not require a SYSGEN procedure; instead it is self-configuring at initial program load (IPL) time. The system designer merely maintains a text file of parameters used to drive the config-uration process as shown in Figure 8-3. A Job Description Language command is provided that allows the system designer to test a new system definition file. This technique relieves the designer of the tedium normally associated with system generation and saves the ex-pense of sending a field engineer to "SYSGEN" the system.

```
*        1         2         3         4         5         6
*2345678901234567890123456789012345678901234567890123456789 0
S  AL  []   1983
***
C C                            ; CPU Board
U ST01      SERIAL/0/0         SRITEK for IBM-PC/XT    ; Main terminal
U ST02      SERIAL/1/0         TVI925, 9600/EVEN/7/1   ; Televideo 925
U BL01      SERIAL/2/0         60/10/15,   2400        ; Async 3780
U DS00      VIRTUAL/0/0        5/5, 4000               ; Virtual 0
U DS01      VIRTUAL/0/1        5/5, 4000               ; Virtual 1
U DS02      VIRTUAL/0/2        5/5, 4000               ; Virtual 2
U DS03      DISK/0/0           5/5, 18000              ; (SRIDEF1.DSK)
U DS04      FLOPPY/0/0         5/5, 640                ; Raw floppy 0
***
P   60000       1              ; Partition 001 -- Terminal ST01
P   60000       1              ; Partition 002 -- Terminal ST02
P   60000       2              ; Partition 101 -- Nonterminal
P       0      99              ; Partition 102 -- Nonterminal
P       0      99              ; Partition 103 -- Nonterminal
P    4000      99              ; Partition 999 -- Shared File
*        1         2         3         4         5         6
*2345678901234567890123456789012345678901234567890123456789 0
```

Figure 8-3   An Example of a System Definition File for the IBM PC. The parameters that are specific to the IBM PC appear only on the controller specification (C) and unit specification (U) records. These records specify the devices attached to the computer. For the initial configuration, the integrated terminal is configured at SERIAL/0/0. This terminal, named ST01, is also the console terminal.

The Job Description Language

Users communicate with RM/COS by means of the Job Description Language (JDL). JDL features include:

1) An interactive command mode.

2) A traditional batch command mode.

3) A hybrid "interactive batch" command mode.

4) Automatic batch upon logon.

5) Command and command parameter abbreviation.

6) Synonym substitution.

In interactive mode, the operator simply enters a command name. The system prompts the operator for the necessary command parameters by displaying the keyword name for each parameter. While this method gives the operator direct control at all times, it is not appropriate for the typical RM/COS end user.

The traditional and the hybrid batch mechanisms are used to "hide" the operating system from the end user. The traditional batch mode uses a disk file of JDL commands (batch stream). In this mode, a command name is followed by a list of keyword parameters, as follows:

```
<cc>/<command-name>[,<keyword>=<value>][<,keyword>=<value>]...
```

Batch mode provides additional commands that control execution within the batch stream, allowing conditional execution and looping. When using traditional batch mode, the values for all parameters must be known before the execution of the batch stream.

The hybrid "interactive batch" stream is an important RM/COS concept. In this mode, the operator may be prompted for some command parameters within the batch stream. The prompts displayed to the operator may be customized by placing the prompt between the keyword and the equal sign, as:

```
<keyword>("<custom prompt>")=(<default value>)
```

Note that a default value may be displayed along with the prompt. If a custom prompt is not present, the keyword itself is used for the prompt.

The automatic batch upon logon feature allows the application designer to generate packages in which the end user never enters any JDL commands. In this mode, the system manager specifies the pathname of a batch stream file that is to be executed immediately after a user successfully logs onto the system.

While not important to the end user, command abbreviation is of importance to the application developer. Any command may be abbreviated by omitting letters from the right end of the command name; as long as the command can be uniquely identified, the abbreviation is valid. Similarly, command parameter keywords may also be abbreviated. For example, the BATCH command—the only command that begins with B— may be abbreviated B, BA, BAT, or BATC.

Finally, RM/COS synonym substitution provides a means to cause one string of characters (usually long or variable) to replace another string of characters (usually short and invariant) within a JDL command before interpreting the command. This substitution allows a single batch stream to be used with varying results, depending on the value of one or more synonyms. Another use of synonyms is to "remember" operator responses when such responses apply to more than one command in a JDL batch stream. (Synonyms may also be used for passing limited amounts of information between COBOL run units, rather than using a file for the same purpose.)

A summary of the JDL commands, grouped by function, is listed in the following paragraphs.

File commands:

1) ASSIGN - Binds a logical name to a file.

2) CHANGE - Changes the characteristics of a file.

3) CREATE - Creates a file.

4) DELETE - Deletes a file.

5) DIRECTORY - Creates a directory file.

6) FCOPY - Copies a file.

7) FILE-BACKUP - Creates a backup/archive copy of a file, subdirectory, or volume.

8) FILE-RESTORE - Restores a file, subdirectory, or volume from a backup.

9) FILE-VALIDATE - Validates a backup created by FILE-BACKUP.

10) INITIALIZE - Initializes a new disk volume.

11) KEY - Predefines indexed file keys (normally performed by COBOL open output).

12) LOAD - Installs a volume so that the operating system may use it.

13) PRINT - Prints a file without using the queuing subsystem.

14) RECLOSE - Repairs a file damaged due to power failure.

15) RELEASE - Releases the binding of a logical name to a file.

16) RENAME - Changes the pathname of a file.

17) REPLACE - Replaces a cataloged file with a scratch file.

18) SCRATCH - Creates a scratch file using the characteristics of a cataloged file.

19) SHOW - Displays a file on the terminal screen.

20) SORT - Performs sort/merge functions.

21) TAPE-ASSIGN - Binds a logical name to a tape file.

22) UNLOAD - Makes a volume unavailable to the operating system.

Batch control commands:

1) BATCH - Starts a new batch stream and waits until completion before executing the next JDL command in the current batch stream. This command can also be used to start a concurrent batch stream in a nonterminal partition.

2) CHAIN - Starts a new batch stream and terminates the current batch stream.

3) LOOP - Defines the beginning of a JDL command loop.

4) REPEAT - Loop closure.

5) REPOINT - Rewinds the batch listing file.

6) SETCOND - Sets the conditional execution control variable.

7) SYNONYM - Defines or deletes a synonym.

8) UNCOUPLE - Breaks the sire/offspring connection between the initiating partition and the execution partition.

Data communication commands:

1) CONNECT - Establishes a logical communications link.

2) FTS - Acts as a SEND or RECEIVE command depending on the remote end of an RM/COS-to-RM/COS link.

3) RECEIVE - Receives a file over a logical link.

4) SEND - Sends a file over a logical link.

Program development and execution commands:

1) COBOL - Invokes the RM/COBOL compiler.

2) COMBINE - Combines the contents of one or more program files into a new program file with optional deletes.

3) EDITOR - Invokes the line editor.

4) EXECUTE - Starts execution of a COBOL run unit.

5) FLAG-PROGRAM - Allows certain nonstandard COBOL treatments.

6) SWITCH - Sets/resets COBOL switches.

Miscellaneous commands:

1) CONTINUE - Continues an interrupted process.

2) EXIT - Terminates an interrupted process.

3) FDUMP - Dumps the (partial) contents of a file.

4) FMODIFY - Modifies the contents of a file.

5) HALT - Interrupts a nonterminal partition process.

6) INSTALL-SYSTEM - Installs a new RM/COS system for use at the next IPL.

7) KPRINTER - Kills the current print file.

8) KTASK - Kills a nonterminal partition process.

9) LIST - Displays the hierarchical directory structure of a volume or subdirectory.

10) MAP-KEYS - Displays statistics about one or more indexed files.

11) MAP-PROGRAMS - Displays statistics about one or more program files.

12) MAP-SYNONYMS - Displays the partition's current synonyms and values.

13) MESSAGE - Sends a message to one or more terminals.

14) PARTITION - Changes the size or scheduling priority of a partition.

15) QUIT - Logs off.

16) REMOVE-SYSTEM - Removes the installed RM/COS system from a volume.

17) SDUMP - Dumps a sector.

18) SMODIFY - Modifies a sector.

19) STATUS - Displays the status of partitions, devices, and logical names.

20) TEST-SYSDEFIL - Allows a new system definition file to be tested at the next IPL.

21) TIME - Sets the system date and time.

22) VARY - Removes a peripheral from service or returns a peripheral to service.

23) VCOPY - Copies a volume to an identical volume.

System Security

Each user may be provided a unique user identification and password that must be entered to gain access to RM/COS. A master user, called the system manager, may use a utility program to maintain the user data base.

Each user identification has an associated privilege level. This privilege level is used to control the use of Job Description Language commands and also to control the use of files in the cataloged file system.

Each Job Description Language command may be entered in either an interactive mode or in a batch mode. However, as an additional security feature, the system designer or system manager may selectively delete certain commands from either the interactive or batch repertoire. In this manner, use of these commands can be restricted to carefully controlled situations.

Cooperating User Processes

The RM/COS operating system has two provisions that allow two or more user processes (i.e., programs), each running in its own partition, to act as cooperating user processes. These provisions are record locking and user event signaling. These features may be used by the applications designer separately or in combination.

A file may be shared among cooperating user processes by designating an access type other than "Exclusive All" (with the ASSIGN JDL command). RM/COS prohibits concurrent modification operations on a shared file (e.g., two WRITEs, two DELETEs, a WRITE and a DELETE, etc.). Concurrent nonmodifying operations (i.e., two or more READs) are allowed. In this manner, the integrity of the file structure is assured when the file is shared.

Record locking is used to prevent simultaneous updates of an individual record. Under RM/COS, a program can lock a record at the time the record is read. Using this feature, the program gains exclusive access to the locked record until the program issues a subsequent I/O operation for the same file (e.g., a rewrite). No other program can access the record while it is locked.

User event signaling may be used by cooperating processes to communicate the occurrence of an event of mutual interest. In the RM/COS environment, user event signaling may be combined with file sharing and record locking to provide event-driven processing. For example, a program modifying a file may notify other programs that a modification has occurred. User event signaling is supported by the COBOL subroutine library package.

User Memory Partitions

The available user memory under RM/COS is divided into segments called **partitions.** Every process must execute in a partition, and each partition can support only one process at a time. All logical name and synonym assignments are local to the partition in which they are made. The size of each partition, the location of each partition in physical memory, and the priority of each partition is defined in the system definition file, but may be changed with the PARTITION command. As JDL commands and applications programs are executed by a user, memory within that user's partition is allocated and de-allocated on an as-needed basis. Under RM/COS, all memory allocation (after IPL) is performed within the partition of the process requesting the memory. This strategy prevents one user's excessive demands for memory from interfering with the correct operation of other users' applications.

There are three types of partitions: terminal, nonterminal, and shared file. Associated with each terminal device is a terminal partition. A terminal partition becomes active when a user logs in at a terminal device; the partition becomes idle when the user QUITs. All but one of the remaining partitions are nonterminal partitions, and may be activated by a BATCH command. The shared file partition is not available to any process. Instead, this partition is available for the memory structures that represent shared disk files (files not assigned exclusively to a single user).

A partition's priority is an integer from 1 to 65535, inclusive. The priority determines what fraction of the available processor time a process executing in the partition receives. A priority of 1 maximizes the processor time available to a process; a higher number reduces the processor time available to a process. If two processes are contending for the processor, the first with a priority of 1 and the second with a priority of 2, the first process will receive twice as much time as the second process. If only one process can use the processor because all other processes are awaiting I/O requests, the running process will receive all of the processor time regardless of its priority.

The File Subsystem

The RM/COS file subsystem is responsible for managing I/O devices and mass storage (disk) files. The file subsystem presents a device independent file interface to the application program.

Each device connected to the system is given a unique four character device name. The first two characters are letters that identify the device type. The last two characters are numerals that specify the device number (e.g., ST01). Device names are bound to specific hardware devices by the system configuration process.

RM/COS disk volumes may be divided into separate files. Files are grouped into sets called directories, which are themselves files. Directories are hierarchically organized into a tree structure having as its root the volume directory. Each file on a disk has a unique designation, called a pathname. A pathname consists of a volume name followed by zero or more directory names and finally followed by a file name. All names within the pathname are separated by periods. Note that within a directory, all file names must be unique; however, two directories may contain the same file name without ambiguity.

The volume name for a disk cartridge is specified using the INITIALIZE command. File names for directory files and nondirectory files are specified by the DIRECTORY and CREATE commands, respectively. The volume directory name may be omitted from the pathname (i.e., the pathname may begin with a period), indicating to

RM/COS that the volume directory of the system disk volume is to be used.

The directory tree structure encourages the designer to group files with related content into a common directory. Such grouping may also provide operational convenience (e.g., copying entire direc- tory structures using FCOPY), depending upon the application.

COBOL applications programs and some Job Description Language commands require logical names to refer to devices or files. Logi- cal names are bound to actual devices or files by using the AS- SIGN, CREATE, CONNECT, or TAPE-ASSIGN commands; the binding is severed by using the RELEASE command.

Each file on an RM/COS disk volume has certain conceptual charac- teristics. These characteristics are used to control the means by which individual logical records are processed and to control the ac- cessibility of files to various applications and users. These charac- teristics are:

   1)   Logical record length.

   2)   Block size.

   3)   Number of blocking buffers.

   4)   Initial disk allocation.

   5)   Secondary disk allocation.

   6)   Organization.

   7)   Type.

   8)   Privilege level.

   9)   Delete protection.

   10)   Write protection.

The logical record length specifies the maximum number of characters that may be contained in a single logical record of the file. The block size specifies the number of characters that are to be con- tained in a logical block. A logical block is the unit of data trans- ferred to or from a disk device in one operation. A logical block may contain one or more logical records and, except for indexed files, may contain only a portion of a logical record.

The number of blocking buffers specifies the amount of a user partition that is to be used, while a file is open, as buffer storage for logical blocks. Within limits, file I/O will use multiple blocking buffers to enhance I/O time at the expense of the additional memory used.

The initial disk allocation and the secondary disk allocation, described in the following paragraphs, specify the amount of physical storage area needed to contain file data.

RM/COS supports the three types of file organization used in COBOL programs: sequential, relative, and indexed. In addition, RM/COS supports three types of file organization for system data: directory, program, and multipartite direct secondary (MDS). The multivolume sequential disk (MVD or MVSD) file organization is intended for use with the FILE-BACKUP and FILE-RESTORE commands. But, COBOL programs may access MVD files in the same manner as sequential files.

There are several RM/COS file types. A file can take on the attributes of one or more of these types. The **spool** type, which applies to sequential organization files only, records slewing information in a transparent manner. The **work** type is specified for files to be written in the deferred write mode. In deferred write mode, file records are not actually written to the disk until the memory space occupied by the records is needed or until the file is closed. The **auto** type is specified for files that are open and updated over long periods of time and require a high degree of data integrity while minimizing the need for data recovery in the event of a power failure or other fault. The **scratch** type is specified for a temporary file. Scratch files are automatically deleted when they are released from a logical name. Scratch files are always treated as work files.

The **compressed** type file occupies less disk space than a normal file. In a compressed file, consecutive repeated characters are encoded as one or two characters before they are written. The original characters are restored to the record after the record is read.

When created, RM/COS files are assigned privilege levels. A privilege level is an integer value in the range of 0 through 65535.

Files may be protected against deletion and/or modification. A write-protected file may be neither deleted nor modified; a delete-protected file may not be deleted. Directories may also be delete-protected.

As stated previously, RM/COS disk volumes may be divided into separate files. RM/COS manages the available storage on a disk volume and allocates storage to files as needed. RM/COS divides a disk volume into units called Allocatable Disk Units (ADU). Each ADU is an integral multiple of physical disk sectors.

When a file is created, two disk allocation parameters are provided describing the initial amount and, if the file size may exceed the initial size, the secondary, or incremental, amount of disk storage required for the file. RM/COS allocates the number of ADUs required for the initial amount of disk storage by first attempting to find a group of contiguous ADUs large enough to satisfy the requirement and then, if no contiguous space is large enough, by finding the smallest number of noncontiguous groups that will satisfy the requirement.

As data is added to a file, the amount of storage in the current allocation may be exhausted. If the secondary allocation creation parameter was nonzero, RM/COS attempts to allocate additional disk storage (sufficient to hold the added data) in increments of the secondary allocation amount. First, if the ADU with a number one higher than the last ADU allocated to the file is unallocated, that ADU (and as many contiguous ADUs as required to satisfy the secondary allocation requirement) will be allocated to the file. If this fails to allocate enough disk storage, a search, identical to the search described for the initial amount, will be made for additional ADUs.

Summary

RM/COS contains the features and utilities that are required for running RM/COBOL applications in a multiuser business environment. The full screen editor, multilevel file directories, the canonical keyboard, spooler, 3780 communications utility, and job control language are all prerequisites in the minicomputer and mainframe environments. RM/COS brings these features to the new multiuser "desktop computer" systems.

The efficiency and speed of RM/COS is directly attributable to its record-oriented design. The record is both the natural unit of information in business data processing and also the fundamental unit for the RM/COS operating system. Additional business software concepts—such as record locking and multikeyed indexed files—are integral to the design and implementation of the RM/COS operating system.

References

RM/COS User Manual, Ryan-McFarland Corporation, 1983.

Thomas H. Morrison is currently a senior member of the technical staff at Ryan-McFarland Corporation. He was previously a member of the staff at the University of Texas Computation Center. At Texas Instruments, he developed software for 990 computer products and the Advanced Scientific Computer. Thomas has a B.S.C.S. from Michigan State University.

Peter H. Ziebelman is the RM/COS product manager at Ryan-McFarland Corporation. Prior to joining Ryan-McFarland, he served as a marketing manager and software product strategy manager in the Semiconductor Group of Texas Instruments. Peter has a B.S. in Combined Sciences from Yale University.

Chapter 9

THE SuperDOS OPERATING SYSTEM

*A Business-oriented Multiuser Operating System
with Data Base Capabilities*

Tom Lee
Bluebird Systems

9

SuperDOS is an efficient multiuser operating system designed by Bluebird Systems specifically for use in the development and operation of sophisticated business applications. This operating system is designed to provide microcomputer programmers with the same power and flexibility as that available to minicomputer programmers. SuperDOS users find that the presence of powerful features normally found only in minicomputer operating systems—coupled with the operating system's speed and ease of use—allow them to easily develop sophisticated business software.

Unlike many operating systems in use today, SuperDOS was conceived, designed and developed by two business applications programmers. Together, the authors have over twenty years of experience in developing end user business applications on minicomputers. Because of their business applications experience, the authors were able to make difficult operating system implementation tradeoffs to ensure speed and efficiency for business software packages.

SuperDOS currently operates on two microprocessors, the Zilog Z80 and the Intel 8088 (the system processor for the IBM PC and XT). As viewed by the user, SuperDOS is identical in both implementations with the exception that SuperDOS can run concurrently with PC-DOS on the IBM PC and XT.

The number of terminals running programs under SuperDOS depends on the particular machine that is being used. On the IBM PC, up to ten terminals can operate concurrently. On the Bluebird II Turbo (hosted by a Z80H processor), 16 terminals can be used.

SuperDOS is written in the native assembly language of the host microprocessor. Although the use of assembly language makes it difficult to transport SuperDOS to other microprocessors, this implementation language choice is one of the primary reasons that SuperDOS is fast and efficient.

Some of the features built into SuperDOS include:

1) The ability to run up to 255 programs concurrently.

2) An extensive file I/O capability that includes the ability to read and write by byte, record, or sector. Also, records can be read sequentially—by record number or by index key.

3) Multi-key indexing that allows any number of index files to reference a data base file. Keys can be added, deleted, and read generically, specifically, or sequentially (forward or backward).

4) A file system that allows multiple programs to access and update files concurrently.

5) A record locking facility.

6) The ability to run a batch stream on any terminal by storing commands on a disk file.

7) "Logical" terminal commands that support many types of terminals with no software changes.

8) The ability of a user on one terminal to start a program on another terminal or to "detach" an executing program and run another program under a different task.

9) Subdirectories and path specifications.

10) Security capabilities that can protect against unauthorized access to the entire system, to specific directories, or to individual files within a directory.

Execution Environment

The entire operating system is always resident and requires approximately 20K bytes of main memory. Another 20K is required for the Business Basic processor. In all Z80 implementations, the hardware must provide bank switching in order to allow more than one task.

When running concurrently with PC-DOS, SuperDOS and Business Basic require a total of 50K bytes of main memory.

SuperDOS also requires interrupt-driven disk controllers and a real-time clock.

User Interface

The SuperDOS interface consists of two parts: signing on to the system and entering command lines. Before any processing can occur in a task, a user must be signed on. To sign on, a user must enter a password. SuperDOS verifies the password by looking it up in the PASSWORD file. If the password is not valid, the user cannot continue.

Once the user has entered a valid password, SuperDOS assigns values for the following user attributes:

1) Security (priority) level. This level ranges from 1 to 7 (7 is the highest level). Security levels are used to restrict file access.

2) User group access. This access information restricts a user to a specific subset of subdirectories.

3) Auto-program. This attribute supplies the name of a program that will start automatically when the user sign-on is complete. If this name is blank, the system prompts the user for a command line.

4) Auto-logoff. If the password starts with a "\", the user is automatically BYE'd (logged off) the system when the prompt character is redisplayed.

Once a user has signed on, he/she interfaces to the system by entering command lines. SuperDOS prompts for a command line by displaying a prompt character (">"). A command line can either be typed in at a terminal, sent to the task from a program that is running in another task, or sent ahead by a program running in the task itself.

A command line is simply a program name followed by any other command information. The program can either be a utility program (supplied with SuperDOS) or a user-written Business Basic or assembly language program. For example,

>TYPE MYFILE

causes the program named TYPE to be loaded. TYPE will display a file ("MYFILE") on the user's terminal. There are no built-in commands in SuperDOS. The user may view such functions as DIR, DEL, and TYPE as commands. But, in reality, each of these functions is a utility program that performs the "command."

Once a program has completed execution, SuperDOS prompts for another command line. Note that a SuperDOS task is either in the process of executing a program or waiting to accept a command line from the user.

Utility Programs

SuperDOS includes a set of utility programs to perform normal system chores—listing file directories, deleting files, moving files, listing file contents, editing text files, examining the free space on a disk, initializing a disk, etc.

Other utilities perform system-specific chores. For example:

1) CONFIGURE - Performs a SYSGEN-type function. CONFIGURE allows the user to specify system parameters in a text file. Such parameters include the maximum number of tasks to run, the maximum number of files to open at one time, the memory size of each task, the type of terminals associated with each task and the default system drive. (CONFIGURE is run automatically as part of the system boot procedure.)

2) MMI - Allows a user to display and change task related information such as default user groups, terminal types, unpend keys, and interrupt keys. MMI also displays all the tasks that are running and allows users with a priority level of 7 to interrupt or halt any of the running tasks.

3) PASSWORDFM - Allows a level 7 user to add, change, and/or delete entries in the PASSWORD file.

The Business Basic Language

At the present time, one high-level language runs under SuperDOS. This language is a compatible superset of Data General's Business Basic language. The language is powerful and flexible—providing the programmer with access to all of the features that are incorporated in SuperDOS. Most of the system's utility programs are written in Business Basic.

Support of Business Basic under SuperDOS opens up access to software written by hundreds of OEM's and installed in over ten thousand business installations.

Bluebird's Business Basic implementation consists of a compiler and a run-time token processor. The token processor resides in the first task and is usually started automatically when the system is booted. In addition to the compiler and run-time processor, there is an inter- active Basic debugger called CODECHEK.

Task Control

Task switching is accomplished by a round robin scheduling scheme. If a task is waiting for an I/O operation to be completed, its time slice is given to the next task in line.

When control is to be switched to another task, the current task's program counter, stack pointer, and register set are saved. The new task's program counter, stack pointer, and register set are restored to the values saved when the task was deactivated. At this point, the new task begins executing and will continue executing until the time slice is exhausted, an I/O operation is started, or the task suspends itself.

As programs are started and stopped, the system dynamically changes the value of the time slice. In this manner, terminal response time is optimized.

Memory Management

SuperDOS uses fixed memory partitions. The size of each partition is normally the same for each task. The partitions are set by the utility program, CONFIGURE. Under a normal implementation, this program is only run when the system is booted.

CONFIGURE reads a disk file containing the size specifications for each task. SuperDOS is distributed with a standard configuration file but the user is free to change the file or create alternate files for special situations.

Fixed memory partitions are used because memory is inexpensive and continually declining in price. Under SuperDOS, to add more users, one need only add more memory. This simplifies the size and overhead of the operating system, which in turn allows more time to be spent processing the user's programs. A typical memory configuration is shown in Figure 9-1.

0-20K	SuperDOS code
	Task Control Blocks and system tables
20-40K	Task #1 information block
	BASIC token processor
40-64K	Task #2 information block
	BASIC re-entrant information
	Task #2 program and variable space
232-256K	Task #9 information block
	BASIC re-entrant information
	Task #9 program and variable space

Figure 9-1 A Typical SuperDOS Memory Configuration.

I/O Management

SuperDOS provides a set of system calls to perform I/O for a variety of peripheral devices. In addition, SuperDOS contains a comprehensive set of disk file I/O calls that provide sophisticated data base management for the user.

SuperDOS supports both serial and parallel character I/O. Character output is processed by interrupt handlers. When a system call is made to perform output, the calling program does not execute (and does not use any of its time slice) until all the characters have been sent.

Input characters are moved to a special "ring" buffer in the task information block by the interrupt service routine. When a system call is made to get input, the characters are removed from the ring buffer and moved to the input buffer specified by the calling program. The ring buffer is 80 bytes in length and can also be filled by system calls. This feature is useful for processing batch streams. A batch program can place input directly into the ring buffer; when the next program needs input, the input characters will already be present in the buffer.

Tape I/O is performed using the XLOAD and XCALL statements provided by Business Basic. These are assembly language subroutine calls that allow 9-track and cartridge tapes to be read, written, rewound, etc.

A utility program is also provided that can backup and restore disk files to and from tape. During backup and/or restore operations, the user can specify all files, all files in one or more subdirectories, or selected filenames. Filenames can include "wild card" characters.

Disk Formats

SuperDOS supports both flexible diskette and hard disk drives. Each disk contains a system information sector, a bit map, a disk directory, and a collection of files.

A logical SuperDOS sector is 512 bytes of disk storage. SuperDOS performs all the necessary adjustments to convert different physical sectors into a 512-byte logical sector. A skewing algorithm is employed to optimize flexible diskette access time; no skewing algorithm is employed for hard disk drives.

The Disk File System

The disk directory contains one entry for each file on the disk. Each file is identified by a name and subdirectory number. A filename can contain up to 12 characters. Only letters, digits, and the characters "/.-" are permitted in a filename. A filename is converted to radix-40 representation for storage in a directory entry—reducing the filename's length to 8 bytes.

The subdirectory number—called a user group—ranges from 0-63. The user group allows different files on the same disk to have the same name. It also provides a method of ensuring file security since a user can be given access to only specific user groups and restricted from all others.

Each directory entry also contains an absolute sector number. This sector number identifies the position of the "header" sector of the file. The first sector of a data file is the next contiguous sector after the file's header sector.

When searching the directory for a filename, a hashing formula is used to determine which directory sector should contain the name. Each directory sector also has one overflow sector. If a filename is not found in the hashed-to sector or in the associated overflow sector, the file is not in the directory—and hence not on the disk.

Disk Files

A disk file is uniquely identified by a drive number, a user group, and a name. When a file is referenced by name only, SuperDOS uses a default drive and user group. The default drive and user group can be modified by the user at any time from within a program or by means of a utility command.

Files in SuperDOS always occupy contiguous sectors on disk. This allocation technique requires that the file size be specified when the file is created. This technique trades off the flexibility to dynamically expand files in favor of fast file access.

SuperDOS supports four file types:

1) Text files. Text files normally contain ASCII characters and are used for word processing documents, source programs, batch commands, etc.

2) Relocatable files. These files are produced by the assembler or compiler. A relocatable file is only used as an object file—to be loaded and run by SuperDOS.

3) Data files. Data files are record-oriented files. When a data file is created, the user specifies a record length. When a read or write is performed, SuperDOS easily calculates the record's location and the record size in bytes. SuperDOS keeps track of deleted records so that disk space can be reused when new records are added.

4) Index files. Index files are files containing keys and pointers to data base records. Any number of index files may exist for a data base. SuperDOS uses a binary tree concept when new keys are added so the keys are always in order. When all keys from an index block are deleted, the entire block is available for reuse. With this technique, index file sorts or reorganizations are not needed. An index file can be searched for an exact match on a key or for a generic (or partial) key. The keys can also be read sequentially in forward or reverse order. Since the keys are always maintained in order and not in an overflow area, a key search is very fast regardless of the key's position in the index file. Areas within an index file are automatically locked by SuperDOS when the file I/O semaphore is used. A key add or delete operation is performed in one pass through the file I/O drivers.

Because every file is contiguous, any file type can be read sequentially or randomly by byte, record, or sector. Also, all files can be processed in the shared mode by any number of users concurrently. Consequently, all files can be locked by record or by sector.

File Security

Each file has a set of protect flags associated with it. A protect flag has a value from 0 to 7. The value of the flags indicates whether or not a particular function can be performed. The flags govern the following functions:

R - Reading information from the file.

W - Writing information to the file.

Create a file.
Delete a file.
Open a file.
Close a file.
Close all files open for a specific task.
Initialize a file.
Check the existence of a file.
Rename a file.
Read one or more records/sectors by record/sector number.
Read one or more records/sectors at the "next" record/sector number.
Read one or more records/sectors at the "previous record/sector number.
Read one or more records by an index file key.
Read one or more records by the "next" key.
Read one or more records by the "previous" key.
Read one or more bytes at a specified byte offset.
Retrieve key information from an index file.
Retrieve the "next" key.
Retrieve the "previous" key.
Update one or more records/sectors by record/sector number.
Update one or more records/sectors by key.
Update one or more bytes at a specified byte offset.
Add a record to a data file.
Add a key to an index file.
Add an index key and a data record.
Retrieve the next available record number.
Delete a record from a data file.
Delete a key from an index file.
Delete an index key and a data record.
Lock one or more records.
Unlock one or more records.
Unlock all records locked by a task.
Allocate a device to a task.
Deallocate a device.
Retrieve a device allocation.
Send a character string to a port.
Read a character string from a port.
Read a single character from a port.
Retrieve a single character from a port if one is ready.
Position cursor to line and column.
Perform one of the 25 logical terminal functions.
Retrieve the characters required to perform a logical terminal function.
Halt a program in a task.
Sign off a user from a task.
Force a program to start in another task.
Chain to another program.
Detach a port from a task.
Attach a task to a port.
Send information to a task's ring buffer (auto-reply).
Suspend a task for 1 cycle.
Suspend a task for a specified time.
Retrieve the current time and date.
Convert between ASCII and radix-40 format.
Convert between ASCII calendar and binary Julian dates.

Table 9-1 SuperDOS System Calls.

D - Deleting or initializing (purging) a file.

M - Modifying the protect flags.

The value of a flag is compared to the user's priority level. (The user's priority level is determined by the password that was used during sign-on.) If the user's priority is less than the value of the protect flag, the user cannot perform the associated function.

In addition to the priority level, the user's password also determines which user groups the user can access. If a user does not have access to a particular user group, the files in that group can not be read, updated, or deleted. Moreover, the names of the files will not even appear in a directory listing.

SuperDOS System Calls

In order to summarize the functionality of SuperDOS, all the SuperDOS system calls are listed in Table 9-1. These calls may be invoked directly from assembly language programs or indirectly from a Business Basic program.

References

SuperDOS Programmer's Guide, Bluebird Systems.

SuperDOS User's Guide, Bluebird Systems.

Tom Lee is a senior systems analyst for Bluebird Systems and the coauthor of SuperDOS and Business Basic. Tom received an M.S. in operations research at UCLA and spent ten years as an applications programmer for Burroughs Corporation and Compusource Corporation. In the Fall of 1979, while working as an independent business applications consultant, Tom teamed up with Dave Houge to develop a microcomputer-based multiuser workstation network. This work led to the development of SuperDOS and Business Basic.

Chapter 10

THE TurboDOS OPERATING SYSTEM

*Software 2000's CP/M-compatible,
Networking Operating System*

Rex Jackson
Arrow Electronics, Inc.

TurboDOS

10

The TurboDOS operating system is Software 2000's flexible and powerful multiuser operating system. It runs on microcomputers that are compatible with the CP/M, the CP/M-86, and the CP-NET operating systems. Because the TurboDOS operating system is compatible with the CP/M operating system, users have access to a large pool of readily-available applications software. TurboDOS can be used as a direct replacement for CP/M on Z80 microcomputer systems and CP/M-86 on 8086-family systems.

The TurboDOS operating system is designed to alleviate many typical microprocessor operating system limitations—especially file size restrictions. Hard disk drives up to one gigabyte (over 1000 megabytes) in size are supported without partitioning. Moreover, random access files may be up to 134 megabytes in length. Extremely large files are not uncommon in business applications. For example, an auto dealership or parts supplier may require upwards of 50M bytes to store information for over 500,000 parts (part number, price, stock level, inventory dates, etc.).

In a network implementation, the TurboDOS operating system accommodates a wide range of network topologies. Networking configurations also provide the interlocks necessary to permit multiuser access to common data bases.

The Human Interface

All TurboDOS file commands have consistent formats and options. For example, the COPY command allows a user to copy a file or a group of files from a "source" to a "destination." (Note that the following example describes only a limited subset of the COPY command options.) COPY options allow the user to request:

1) A query for each file. This option gives the user control over each individual file to be copied (e.g., when a wild card filename is used).

2) A prompt if the destination file already exists. This option allows the user to delete the existing file, if desired.

3) That all files be copied without operator intervention —automatically deleting any files that already exist.

COPY also allows a user to copy from one user area to another (if the privilege codes permit). For example,

    COPY B:*.COM C: ;N S2 D5

copies all files with file extension ".COM" from the source—drive B ("B:"), user 2 ("S2")—to the destination—drive C ("C:"), user 5 ("D5").

System Support

All unique TurboDOS functions are called using a special TurboDOS entry point, different from the CP/M-family entry point. By using different entry points, any conflict in function call assignments between CP/M and TurboDOS is eliminated. All unique TurboDOS functions are invoked by a call to location 80 on the Z80 and by interrupt 225 on the 8086. Each TurboDOS function is assigned a function number between 0 and 41.

All CP/M BDOS functions and all direct BIOS calls are fully supported. In addition, TurboDOS also provides compatibility with CP/M Plus, MP/M II, and Concurrent CP/M in file and record locks, system date and time, and several other selected areas.

The TurboDOS operating system is also media-compatible with the CP/M operating system. TurboDOS automatically determines whether a diskette is written in standard CP/M format or in Turbo-DOS format. (TurboDOS-formatted diskettes typically run faster and store more data.) The format of a newly-created diskette is determined when the diskette is initialized.

Networking

Networking TurboDOS supports a multiuser network of interconnected microcomputers that can share a common pool of mass storage devices,

printers, and other peripherals. Since there is a microcomputer dedicated to each user, TurboDOS is able to support a large number of simultaneous users with excellent performance and minimal interaction.

Each network processor may have its own local console, printer, and/or
disk drives. Or, a network processor can rely completely on the peripherals attached to other network processors—even the operating system may be downloaded over the network.

TurboDOS accommodates a wide variety of network topologies, from the
simplest master/slave systems to the most complex star, ring, and
hierarchical networks. The network protocol is a simple one, adaptable
to both point-to-point and multidrop links (parallel or serial, polled
or autonomous). Bidirectional (master-to-master) network dialogue—
in which two processors on the network may simultaneously access disks
attached to the other processor—is supported by TurboDOS. TurboDOS
supports any mix of Z80 and 8086-family slave processors in a single
network.

Networking configurations of TurboDOS provide the file and record
interlocks necessary to permit multiuser access to common data bases.
Password-type logon security prevents unauthorized access and pro-
tects private file libraries. A log file keeps an automatic record
of all system usage. TurboDOS provides FIFOs (similar to UNIX pipes)
for interprocess synchronization and interuser communication. Turbo-
DOS supports a sophisticated multiqueue print spooler that allows any
number of users to share a maximum of sixteen printers per processor.

Networking TurboDOS incorporates an advanced failure detection and
recovery facility that makes the system virtually crashproof. Even
a user with malicious intent cannot compromise the processing of
files belonging to another user.

Bank Switching

For Z80 systems, TurboDOS supports 128K bytes of bank switched
memory (two 64K-byte banks). The operating system and a large
pool of disk buffers are located in one bank. The other bank
is divided into a 63K-byte transient program area and a 1K-byte
reserved area. The 63K-byte transient program area provides
considerably more application program space than unbanked configurations of either CP/M or TurboDOS.

Modular Architecture

Modular architecture is one of the most important features of the TurboDOS operating system. TurboDOS is packaged as a set of relocatable modules—each functional area of the operating system and each hardware-dependent device driver are packaged as a separate module. Some of the TurboDOS functional modules include:

1) Command language interpreter.

2) Network request manager.

3) Buffer manager.

4) Spooler/despooler.

5) File manager.

6) Multitask dispatcher.

These modules are building blocks that can be combined in various ways to produce a family of compatible operating systems, including single task, spooling, multitask, real-time, time-sharing, distributed processing, and networking operating systems.

Since each hardware-dependent element is a separate relocatable module, adapting TurboDOS to various hardware configurations is simple and straightforward. Any or all of the modules may be changed easily, without having to perform massive reassemblies or use complex system generation procedures.

There are three TurboDOS system software levels:

1) Process Level. TurboDOS supports multiple processes for user commands/programs, for printer spooling, and for disk buffering operations.

2) Kernel Level. The kernel contains the software that provides approximately one hundred system functions and controls process scheduling, peripheral I/O, and the file system.

3) Driver Level. This level consists of the driver software modules that interface the TurboDOS operating system to the microcomputer hardware (e.g., terminals, printers, disk drives, and a real-time clock).

Performance

Much of the speed advantage of TurboDOS is achieved by means of a sophisticated buffer manager. This module performs multilevel disk I/O buffering, using a least-recently-used (LRU) buffer assignment algorithm and other I/O optimizations. Buffering greatly reduces the number of physical disk accesses in both sequential and random operations. The number and size of buffers are user-defined and can be changed dynamically by using a utility program or by executing an operating system call.

In addition to ordinary CP/M-compatible linear directories, TurboDOS also supports an optional "hashed" directory format. By using a hashing algorithm, the speed of directory lookup operations is significantly increased. Although a hashed directory may be used on any disk, it is especially suited for use on hard disks with large directories.

Additional speed is provided by a program load optimizer. This module scans the allocation map of program files that are to be loaded into memory, determines the sequentially allocated segments of the file (often 16K or more in length), and loads these segments at the maximum transfer rate of the disk controller.

Other major performance improvements are the elimination of warm start and disk logon delays in TurboDOS. Warm start is instantaneous in TurboDOS because the command interpreter is resident. Disk logon is not required in TurboDOS because the allocation map for each disk is stored on the disk and need not be repeatedly recreated in memory.

Disk Capacity

Business applications are often limited by the available disk capacity of microcomputer systems. Most of the increased diskette capacity of TurboDOS is achieved through the use of larger physical sector sizes on the diskette. For example, an ordinary 8-inch, single-sided, single-density diskette can accommodate eight 512-byte sectors per track. With standard 128-byte sectors, on the other hand, 26 sectors can be stored on each track. Thus, 512-byte sectors provide 23% more storage on each track (4096 bytes versus 3328 bytes). Additional capacity is achieved by eliminating reserved "system tracks" (required by many other operating systems).

TurboDOS was designed to take advantage of large hard disks. TurboDOS supports hard disk drives to one gigabyte without partitioning. Individual random access files can be 134 megabytes in length.

Increased Reliability

TurboDOS performs read-after-write verification of all disk update operations. While this type of verification has long been standard practice on large-scale computer systems, it has been virtually unknown among low-cost microcomputer systems. The sophisticated buffer management techniques of TurboDOS make this verification possible without increasing disk access times to intolerable levels.

Whenever errors are detected, TurboDOS provides meaningful diagnostic messages and a variety of recovery options. For example, in the event of a disk error, the operator is prompted to retry the disk operation, to accept the error and continue processing, or to abort the program.

The allocation map for each disk is maintained by TurboDOS on the disk itself. Therefore, a disk can be changed at any time without fear that the disk will become "read-only" or that the data will be compromised. TurboDOS senses and automatically adapts to changes of disk format (single- or double-sided, single- or double-density, etc.). Hassle-free disk changes under TurboDOS make low-cost single-disk systems practical.

TurboDOS includes more than forty common transient processes. Some of these processes include:

1) AUTOLOAD - Allows automatic program execution at each cold or warm start.

2) BACKUP - Provides fast track-by-track copying of similar disks (with verification).

3) BUFFERS - Allows a user to change the number and/or size of disk buffers. In this manner, TurboDOS can be "tuned" for optimum performance.

4) CHANGE - Facilitates disk changes during multiuser operation.

5) COPY, RENAME, and DELETE - Provide the means to copy, rename and delete indivdual files or groups of files. All three utilities support wild card filenames and allow optional confirmation of individual file operations. COPY also allows incremental backup of hard disk files to one or more flexible diskettes.

6) DATE - Allows a user to display and/or set the system date and time.

7) DIR - Displays an alphabetized disk directory in columnar format on either the console or the printer. Full or selective directories may be requested.

8) DO - Initiates the automatic execution of a file of commands. DO-files in TurboDOS may be nested to any reasonable depth and may contain any number of substitution parameters (each with an optional default value).

9) DRIVE - Displays on the console or printer the following disk format information: data capacity, directory size, block size, sector size, sectors per track, number of tracks, and number of reserved tracks.

10) DUMP and TYPE - Display the contents of a file on the console or printer.

11) ERASEDIR - Initializes a disk directory and selects a hashed or linear directory format.

12) FIFO - Permits the creation of a first-in-first-out structure based in RAM or on disk. TurboDOS FIFOs (similar to UNIX pipes) are useful for interprocess synchronization and interuser communication.

13) FORMAT - Performs initialization of diskettes in CP/M or TurboDOS formats.

14) LABEL - Allows a user to label a disk volume.

15) LOGON and LOGOFF - Provide password security, and at the option of the system manager, provide a time/date record of all movements through user areas along with a record of LOGONs and LOGOFFs.

16) MASTER - Allows a network slave console to act as the master console.

17) PRINT, PRINTER, and QUEUE - Permit the operator to control print routing and spooling. TurboDOS supports up to 16 concurrent printers.

References

TurboDOS User's Guide, Software 2000, 1984.

Z80 TurboDOS Programmer's Guide, Software 2000, 1984.

8086 TurboDOS Programmer's Guide, Software 2000, 1984.

Z80 TurboDOS Implementer's Guide, Software 2000, 1984.

8086 TurboDOS Implementer's Guide, Software 2000, 1984.

Rex Jackson became involved in digital electronics repair and training while in the Air Force in 1971. He received a B.S.E.E. degree from the University of Missouri, Columbia while working for the university designing small computer systems. Rex joined Texas Instruments as product engineer for the Memory Group and was software product manager for the Microprocessor Group at Texas Instruments. He currently is with Arrow Commercial Computer Products Group of Arrow Electronics, Denver, Colorado.